Emotion Regulation for Young People with Eating Disorders

Emotion Regulation for Young People with Eating Disorders is a supportive guide for professionals to help them build effective therapeutic relationships with young people struggling with eating disorders.

The book focuses on the role of emotion regulation in the development and maintenance of eating disorders. The psychological concepts discussed are an integration of ideas and theories that have been proposed by many psychologists over the last half-century. The tasks presented in the book use aspects of these theories and concepts in an applied way, which can be helpful to enable young people to understand more about their emotional experience and how it has contributed to their difficulties. The approach proposed can be used across the spectrum of eating disorders as the dysfunctional emotional regulation difficulty is shared by all eating disorders.

The workbook will be helpful for Children and Adolescent Mental Health Services (CAMHS) professionals such as psychiatrists, psychologists, counsellors, nurses, occupational therapists, dieticians and therapeutic care workers.

Sophie Nesbitt is a clinical psychologist working with young people with eating disorders in both inpatient and outpatient settings.

Lucia Giombini is a clinical psychologist and researcher working with young people and adults with eating disorders in Europe and the UK.

Emotion Regulation for Young People with Eating Disorders

A Guide for Professionals

Sophie Nesbitt
Lucia Giombini

LONDON AND NEW YORK

First published 2022
by Routledge
2 Park Square, Milton Park, Abingdon, Oxon OX14 4RN

and by Routledge
605 Third Avenue, New York, NY 10158

Routledge is an imprint of the Taylor & Francis Group, an informa business

© 2022 Sophie Nesbitt and Lucia Giombini

The right of Sophie Nesbitt and Lucia Giombini to be identified as authors of this work
has been asserted by them in accordance with sections 77 and 78 of the Copyright,
Designs and Patents Act 1988.

All rights reserved. No part of this book may be reprinted or reproduced or utilised
in any form or by any electronic, mechanical, or other means, now known or
hereafter invented, including photocopying and recording, or in any information
storage or retrieval system, without permission in writing from the publishers.

Trademark notice: Product or corporate names may be trademarks or registered trademarks,
and are used only for identification and explanation without intent to infringe.

British Library Cataloguing-in-Publication Data
A catalogue record for this book is available from the British Library

Library of Congress Cataloging-in-Publication Data
A catalog record has been requested for this book

ISBN: 978-0-367-47128-6 (hbk)
ISBN: 978-0-367-47127-9 (pbk)
ISBN: 978-1-003-03364-6 (ebk)

Typeset in Helvetica
by Newgen Publishing UK

In loving memory of Professor Bryan Lask

We would like to dedicate this book to Professor Bryan Lask. Bryan brought us together as colleagues and we feel it is what we learnt from him that enabled the idea for this book to develop. In his work Bryan always took a very person-focused approach, starting where the young person wanted to start and not necessarily where the book told you to. He encouraged us as clinicians to be brave in our work and engage in the emotional experience with the young person so we can truly empathise with their distress and help them find meaning to it. Bryan was always very keen to enable the young person and the colleagues he worked with to use themselves within the work. This approach, whilst challenging at times was inspiring and moving. It represented the core principal of therapy, as a two-way experience where both the therapist and the patient will change and discover something new about themselves.

Contents

About the authors	xi
Foreword	xiii
Acknowledgements	xvii

1 Understanding emotional experience as a window towards recovery from eating disorders — 1

Introduction	2
The purpose of the workbook	2
When and how should the book be used?	3
Issue of confidentiality	4
Eating disorders	5
Overview	5
Treatment approaches	6
Workbook approach	8
Personal motivations	9

2 Psychological distress and emotional experience in eating disorders — 13

Overview	14
Understanding psychological distress	16
Basic human needs	16
Psychological distress	19
The development of psychological distress	20
Psychological distress in eating disorders	24
Experiencing psychological distress: deficit or resource?	26
The dandelion and orchid metaphor	28
The emotional journey from childhood to adolescence	33
The role of emotions	33
Childhood	34
Attunement and attachment	34
Gender	36
Food and communication	38
Adolescence	39
Parental relationships	39
Peers and identity	42
Adolescence and body image	43

vii

Contents

Emotion difficulties in eating disorders............45
Emotions in the treatment of eating disorders...........45
Eating disorder symptoms and dysfunctional emotional regulation...........48
Helping young people to connect with their emotional experience...........51

3 Therapy, clinical challenges and the world as a patient   57
Overview...........58
On therapy...........59
Understanding the emotional and social aspects of eating...........59
The experience of therapy and the therapeutic alliance......62
The value of narratives...........67
Challenges of working with young people with eating disorders...........71
Family involvement...........71
Weight preoccupation...........75
The importance of body and mind connections in adolescence...........79
Personality characteristics – perfectionism...........82
Supportive language and feelings in therapists, young people and carers...........87
Stages of recovery – dealing with anger and regression....87
Understanding the importance of therapists' feelings and sensitivity...........90
Understanding the effect of praising in children...........93
The world as a patient...........96
The ideal child and the sensitive child...........96
Psychotherapy of a pandemic...........100
Understanding and promoting resilience...........102
Pandemic and eating disorders...........104
Rethinking mental health: ecopsychology...........108

Contents

4 Exploring the emotional experience in eating disorders: guiding principles and notes for therapists to work with young people   113

Overview 115

Section 1 – Starving emotions 120

Overview. 120

Task 1.1: Identifying emotions 122

Task 1.2: Life without emotions 124

Task 1.3: Why do we need emotions? 127

Task 1.4: How do we recognise emotions? 129

Task 1.5: Expressing your emotions into words 132

Section 2 – The eating disorder filter. 137

Overview. 137

Task 2.1: Setting the scene of your eating disorder 139

Task 2.2: Behind the scenes 142

Task 2.3: Keeping up the performance 144

Task 2.4: The eating disorder magnifying glass 147

Task 2.5: Removing the eating disorder filter 149

Section 3 – Making your playlist. 156

Overview. 156

Task 3.1: Making your playlist 159

Task 3.2: Unexpected scenes 161

Task 3.3: Watching the highlights. 163

Task 3.4: Different versions of your playlist 165

Task 3.5: Connecting to your playlist 167

Section 4 – New playlist, new self. 171

Overview. 171

Task 4.1: Rebranding your playlist 172

Task 4.2: New content in your playlist 174

Task 4.3: How would other people hear your playlist? 176

Task 4.4: Sharing your playlist 178

Task 4.5: Presenting your own self. 179

Contents

Section 5 – Breaking free from the eating disorder filter 183
    Overview. 183
    Task 5.1: Emotional talk with your family 185
    Task 5.2: Rebuilding connections with your peers 187
    Task 5.3: Respect your comfort zone 189
    Task 5.4: Future aspirations 190
    Task 5.5: Private place 192

Index   199

About the authors

Sophie Nesbitt is a Clinical Psychologist who has specialised in working with young people suffering from eating disorders. Sophie completed her clinical training at the University of Leicester. Sophie's first book *Hunger for Understanding – A Motivational Workbook for Young People with Eating Disorders* (Wiley, 2005) has become a valuable resource for many eating disorder practitioners. Sophie has worked in both specialist outpatient and inpatient services working closely with young people and families. As part of Sophie's work, she has contributed to the development of services for young people with eating disorders. She has written on a number of subjects relating to therapeutic treatments. Sophie is passionate about enabling young people to access therapeutic treatments and overcome the challenges and stigma that mental health issues such as eating disorders can create.

Lucia Giombini is a Clinical Psychologist who has worked with both young people and adults suffering from eating disorders. In Italy, Lucia worked for the Italian Ministry of Health on a national research project focusing on the predictive factors and psychopathological dimensions of young people with eating disorders. Following her move to London, Lucia has continued to conduct clinical and research work. In her clinical work she values the therapeutic relationship as the cornerstone of the unique recovery and self-development journey for each person. Lucia's current research, in collaboration with the Institute of Psychiatry, Psychology and Neuroscience, King's College London, is focusing on understanding cognitive and emotional processes and exploring therapy approaches in eating disorders.

About the authors

Josephine Sama is a Therapeutic Art & Play Practitioner working with young people living with eating disorders. She is also a published artist with vast experience in the creative industries, including commissions from notable titles including *Glamour*, *Elle Girl* and *Psychologies* magazines. Josephine is passionate about developing her practice by utilising the power of creativity to enhance the therapeutic experience.

Foreword

Eating disorders can have a devastating impact on the lives of the people they affect, and sadly anorexia nervosa is a psychiatric disorder with the one of the highest mortality rates. Alongside this, it is well documented that within eating disorders generally the carer burden is high and underestimated. Working in the field of eating disorders inevitably means dealing with the challenges of working with this devastating illness, which can take the form of young people and adults becoming physically and emotionally unwell. The illness can impact every aspect of development – physical, emotional, social and academic, often meaning that young people are not able to reach their full potential.

The onset of eating disorders generally occurs during adolescence, which is a critical period of emotional development. Adolescents can be more vulnerable to mental health illness as during this stage of development their brains are particularly amenable to change and the effects of positive experiences and psychological interventions. Emotion regulation difficulties contribute to relapse, supporting the idea that treatment for eating disorders may be enhanced by a specific focus on emotion regulation. Research evidence suggests that people with eating disorders experience difficulties with regulating emotion, and they often develop unhelpful ways to manage emotions such as avoidance, suppression, inhibition, repression, emotion-focused coping, rumination and self-destructive behaviours. The eating disorder symptoms become a way to help manage the overwhelming emotional experiences and communicate emotional distress.

In the past few years, I have had the pleasure to collaborate with Lucia Giombini and Sophie Nesbitt in adapting Cognitive

Foreword

Remediation Therapy and Emotion Skills Training for young people, an approach which was originally developed for adults. The focus of the work has been to apply the experimental research work in cognitive and emotional processing to clinical practice. One of the aims of our work is to help young people to recognise and tolerate their emotions and incorporate the skills learnt in the therapy sessions to everyday life. This is conducted through the use of visual material and simple exercises. It is intended to be a collaborative exploration of the young person's thinking and emotional processing styles, giving the patient basic language and skills to understand, manage and express their emotions. It provides a safe, easy and playful environment where exercises are viewed as fun and easy to experiment with and help young people to begin accessing their emotions.

This new workbook provides an overview of the role of emotion regulation in the development and maintenance of eating disorders. Sophie and Lucia are both experienced clinical psychologists and they bring the research and clinical findings directly into the therapy room. The psychological concepts discussed in the book are an integration of ideas and theories that have been developed by psychologists over the last half-century. Sophie and Lucia describe how eating disorder symptoms can result from young people's difficulties to integrate social and individual needs and acknowledge their own emotional experience. They invite us to take into account the peculiar characteristics and temperament of the person, with a specific focus on biological sensitivity. It is important to consider that each young person can respond differently to situational and relational scenarios based on where they are in the sensitivity trait continuum, in other words on their temperament. The family and the broader social context are

Foreword

explored as well with recommendations for parents and their role in supporting the therapy process of their children, and also with references to how the current global pandemic is impacting young people's lives.

The first three chapters cover the purpose and background to the text, its theoretical bases and a discussion of common challenges to the therapeutic work encountered with young people. To help make the conversation about emotions as simple as possible, the last chapter guides therapists in supporting young people to start exploring their emotions through a series of tasks. Sophie and Lucia use case studies informed by their clinical experience to enrich the understanding and use of the tasks. In many ways it is important that the idea of concluding the tasks does not take over, rather, it is a step-by-step process that evolves over time and that sessions don't necessarily have to be planned around "working through tasks" rather the focus is on the relationship with the tasks as being very helpful to discussion and reflection. The authors highlight how the eating disorder difficulties can be explored in the context of a safe therapeutic relationship with the overall aim of improving the young person's insight into their emotional experience of the world and how this is shaping their responses to emotional pain leading to symptoms of distress.

The approach proposed in the workbook can be used across the spectrum of eating disorders including anorexia nervosa, bulimia nervosa and binge eating disorder, as the dysfunctional emotional regulation difficulties are shared by all eating disorders. The authors support professionals, based on their experience and clinical practice, to establish a therapeutic dialogue with the young people, with the hope that this will make therapists' experience less overwhelming.

Foreword

The workbook is a valuable resource for professionals working in the field of eating disorders for the first time, as the tasks are comprehensive and written in a step-by-step nature. It also might be valuable for multidisciplinary healthcare professionals who have been asked to conduct a short-term and focused piece of work and might value having a structure for their sessions. It could be helpful in particular when working with those young people who are not feeling ready yet to get better, that are maybe at a pre-contemplation/contemplation stage of change, or perhaps young people who find it difficult to engage in a dialogue with a therapist, or may have had a therapy experience that they don't think was helpful. Professionals working within this field often feel overwhelmed and deskilled by the severity of eating disorders' presentations, and often feel at a loss as to how to reach this treatment-resistant group of young people. It is hoped that this workbook becomes a valuable tool to help them.

Sophie and Lucia dedicate this workbook to Professor Bryan Lask who devoted his career to improve understanding and treatment for young people with eating disorders and to support their families. By continuing to conduct in-depth research and clinical work to promote young people's wellbeing they honour his legacy with the hope to enrich young people's lives.

Professor Kate Tchanturia, FBPS, FHEA, FAED

Consultant Clinical Psychologist

King's College London,

Psychological Medicine and

South London and Maudsley NHS Foundation Trust, Eating Disorders National Service

London, November 2020

Acknowledgements

We would like to thank all of the young people and families who have shared their life journey with us, we value their openness and honesty at such difficult times in their lives. Despite the fact that they have to remain anonymous, the conversations we have had with them have shaped us as clinicians and impacted significantly on our working lives. We would also like to thank our colleagues who have been a continued source of support within our own journey of learning and development.

Chapter 1
Understanding emotional experience as a window towards recovery from eating disorders

Introduction   2
  The purpose of the workbook   2
  When and how should the book be used?   3
  Issue of confidentiality   4
Eating disorders   5
  Overview   5
  Treatment approaches   6
  Workbook approach   8
  Personal motivations   9

Introduction

The purpose of the workbook

Research suggests that working with adolescents therapeutically can be difficult, which combined with the treatment-resistant nature of eating disorders makes working within this field both challenging and rewarding. We also know that eating disorders can have a devastating impact on the sufferer and family members. Throughout the duration of the illness young people and their families are often offered a range of treatments. This can lead to therapy fatigue and thus engaging young people in meaningful therapeutic work can be daunting for many therapists. It has been well-recognised that young people struggle to engage in meaningful relationships and find it hard to express their emotions, independently from the treatment approach. Understanding more about how to build effective relationships with young people with eating disorders becomes very important in terms of engaging them in therapeutic work.[1]

This workbook focuses on the exploration and understanding of the emotional experience in the treatment of eating disorders. In terms of structure, there are four chapters in the book. Chapter one offers a broad introduction to eating disorders and chapter two presents a theoretical basis exploring the role of the emotional experience in eating disorders. Chapter three presents a discussion of the importance of therapeutic engagement and communication within this group of young people. Within chapter three we have used clinical material in the form of vignettes; by adding these case studies into the workbook we hope to support the reader to understand how some of the concepts can be applied in the therapeutic work. Finally, chapter four provides a package of practical tools to help therapists engage young people with eating disorders in thinking about their own emotional experience and the role it plays in their difficulties.

All chapters of the book are important for the reader, as it is the concepts shared in both chapter two and chapter three that provide the guidance that will enable the effective delivery of the practical tools described in chapter four. Throughout chapter four, there are sections entitled "Notes for therapists", however, this applies broadly to all practitioners working with young people regardless of therapeutic background or training. The language used is accessible to all disciplines.

When and how should the book be used?

The workbook has been written for practitioners working with young people with eating disorders. The psychological concepts discussed in the book are an integration of ideas and theories that have been proposed by many psychologists over the last half-century. They are well established and may be familiar to many professions working in the field of mental health regardless of training background. In line with National Institute for Health and Care Excellence (NICE) Guidance recommendations for the treatment of eating disorders,[2] the approach outlined in the book should be delivered in the context of multidisciplinary teamwork, with different practitioners managing different aspects of the care and risk assessment. For example, it would not be helpful for the practitioner delivering the therapy to be focusing on weight management as we don't emphasise addressing weight and shape concerns as the main part of the work. Instead, the approach focuses on the physical and psychological experience of the emotions as a window for the young person to explore their individual and social needs as an essential part of their journey towards recovery and self-development.

In the context of the book, we have used the term "psychological distress" to refer to the collection of symptoms that combine to form a diagnosis of an eating disorder. This includes physical symptoms such as weight loss/gain or disruption of hunger drive, cognitive symptoms such as preoccupations with weight and shape or self-critical/self-disgust attitudes and behavioural symptoms such as restriction or bingeing/purging. The approach that we are proposing in the workbook can be used across the spectrum of eating disorders including anorexia nervosa, bulimia nervosa and binge eating disorder or subclinical eating disorders as the dysfunctional emotional regulation difficulties are shared by all eating disorder presentations/diagnoses.

In terms of context, the approach described in the workbook could be useful in both inpatient and outpatient settings, within key work or therapy sessions. As with all clinical work, clinical supervision is important for effective delivery and sufficient reflection and learning on the part of the therapist/practitioner. In terms of a time frame to cover all aspects of chapter four, ideally, we propose between twenty and thirty sessions, however, this may need to be carefully considered in relation to the resources available. With this in mind, it may be necessary to consider which tasks are most relevant. This will be dependent on a clinical judgement based on knowledge of the young person. Some tasks may be helpful for building therapeutic engagement initially, whilst other activities may be used further into the therapeutic process.

Issue of confidentiality
Any therapeutic work undertaken with the workbook should be considered in the context of the therapeutic relationship and all normal conditions of confidentiality should apply. As with

all therapeutic work issues around confidentiality, the limits of this should be explained prior to the beginning of the work. This should be clearly documented in the clinical notes in line with best practice. In relation to feedback to the wider team, this should be discussed and considered within the context of the work taking into account the young person's views. It is also useful for therapists to consider how feedback might be shared with parents and carers. This too needs to be discussed with the young person taking into account their views and their age. In terms of any written work produced the young person and the therapist should agree on how the work is going to be kept safe.

Eating disorders

Overview

Research suggests that the prevalence of eating disorders is increasing, affecting more and more young people. The overall lifetime prevalence of eating disorders among adolescent girls ranges from 3% to 13% and from 1.2% to 1.5% among boys. In girls, the lifetime prevalence of anorexia nervosa ranges from 0.3% to 2.6%, bulimia nervosa from 0% to 2.6%, and binge eating disorder from 1.0% to 3.0%.[3]

The age at which difficulties start tends to be lower, impacting on long term prognosis and increasing the need for differential treatments. There has also been some movement within the male/female ratio, with the number of young men diagnosed with eating disorders increasing. Whilst "binge-eating" behaviours and compensatory behaviours (e.g. purging, fasting, excessive exercise) have a low prevalence in young patients, a "continuum" between bulimia nervosa and anorexia nervosa exists, with a frequent transition from one disorder to another. Over recent years there has been an increased prevalence of eating disorders in young people alongside other psychiatric conditions such as depression, anxiety or obsessive-compulsive disorder. In addition, the diagnostic criteria as set out in DSM-V[4] do not include aspects of the illness that are well known to exist, such as neuropsychological disturbances (e.g. ruminations and obsessions about weight, shape and eating and personality traits such as perfectionism and impulsivity)[5].

Most eating disorders emerge during adolescence, a critical time for brain development, and malnutrition can negatively impact treatment outcomes and recovery. The biological impact of malnutrition is due not only to weight and shape concerns but is also maintained through issues of perfectionism and low self-esteem and self-confidence. Fairburn and colleagues[5] have proposed a model suggesting there are common factors that are present across all eating disorders' diagnostic categories. Understanding eating disorders in this way is referred to as the transdiagnostic approach. It is important to note that transdiagnostic approaches and disorder-focused approaches need not be mutually exclusive and that a "spectrum" model based on an impulse-control paradigm of eating disorders can be informative. We think this is particularly helpful in relation to the approach taken in this book, which thinks of eating disorders as a broader range of difficulties. In this book, we focus on thinking and emotional styles that are common in eating disorders more broadly[5].

Treatment approaches

There are various treatments proposed for eating disorders. The NICE[2] guidance summarises these treatments together and evaluates the evidence base for each. With regard to this, NICE[2] recommends the following psychological interventions be considered for young people with eating disorders: focused family therapy for children and young people with anorexia nervosa or bulimia nervosa (FT-AN/FT-BN). This approach aims to engage the family in helping the person to recover and is a step-by-step treatment. The first step aims to build a good therapeutic alliance with the individual, their parents or carers and other family members. Step two is to support the young person to establish a level of independence appropriate for their level of development with help from their parents or carers. Finally, the third step focuses on plans for when treatment ends and on relapse prevention.

Currently, this type of approach is most commonly offered in a community outpatient setting. For many it is helpful, but some families will struggle to engage effectively in this type of treatment. In these instances, NICE[2] recommends two other forms of treatment: individual cognitive behaviour therapy, which is eating disorder focused (CBT-ED) or adolescent-focused psychotherapy for anorexia nervosa (AFP-ED). These approaches aim to reduce the risk to physical health and any other symptoms of the eating disorder.

CBT-ED focuses on encouraging the young person to reach a healthy body weight through the process of healthy eating. Therapy work undertaken covers psychoeducation relating to nutrition, cognitive restructuring, emotional regulation, social skills, body image concern, self-esteem and relapse prevention. The therapy needs to be mindful of the young person's specific development needs, whilst enhancing self-efficacy, and promoting self-monitoring of dietary intake and associated thoughts and feelings.

Understanding emotional experience

AFP-ED is different from the CBT-ED, as it focuses more on emotions and interpersonal processes, and how these affect the eating disorder. The therapy aims to develop a shared understanding of the young person's psychological issues and how they use anorexic behaviour as a coping strategy and supporting the young person to find alternative strategies for them to manage stress. In later stages of treatment, issues relating to identity and independence can also be explored.

Psychological treatment for binge eating disorder in young people involves the use of cognitive behavioural self-help materials. The aim is to promote engagement in a binge-eating-disorder-focused guided self-help programme. If this approach is not helpful, group CBT-ED, focusing on psychoeducation and self-monitoring of the eating behaviour, is recommended. This approach encourages the young person to think actively about their problems and identify goals. This includes engaging in behavioural techniques such as daily food plans, identifying binge eating cues, body exposure training and helping the person to identify and change negative beliefs about their body. Where a group approach is not available or is declined, individual CBT-ED should be considered.

Workbook approach

Alongside evidence-based treatments, there are also several manualised workbooks available. Some of the workbooks focus on a specific type of eating disorder in line with diagnostic criteria defined by NICE[2] Guidance. The approach explored in this workbook focuses on exploring emotions and the link with eating disorders symptoms. This workbook can be used with young people struggling with any aspect of an eating disorder as the theoretical concepts explored are not dependent on diagnosis. Research[1] has suggested that some therapeutic approaches are too focused on weight and symptom management, which may lead to patients feeling not truly understood in terms of their psychological distress.

This workbook does not address the symptoms directly but rather focuses on the underlying psychological distress, by prioritising the emotional experience of the young person. From the young person's perspective, this approach will hopefully enable them to understand that their symptoms were a representation of something integral to their own experience of the world, which may need to be altered to enable them to thrive. It is hoped that this approach enables the therapist to hold in mind both the individual and social needs of a person that are key to any treatment as it represents the core elements of self that can be seen as a fundamental psychological basis of emotional wellbeing.

Personal motivations

We thought it might be helpful to explain our own personal motivations for writing this book. After many years of working in services, both inpatient and outpatient, as clinicians we felt that we wanted to add something to the existing body of literature that did not focus directly on weight or symptom management. We have really valued the idea of focusing on the emotional experience of the illness and the connections between the body and mind, and how these contribute to the suffering that our patients experience. This approach embodies a much more experiential and interpretative way of working but isn't psychodynamic in its purest form, which can sometimes be off-putting and confusing for practitioners who feel they need some form of therapeutic tool or knowledge to support the work. As practitioners working in the field, we have noticed the need to help young people really understand their emotional experience relating to their suffering rather than just focusing on symptom management. Those young people who have been able to access a more emotional understanding of their illness have been more open to therapy to explore their symptoms. As therapists, accompanying a young person on a journey such as this is very personal and at times moving. It is a process that has inspired and encouraged us to continue to work in the eating disorders field where therapy burnout can be very high as relapse prevention is such a risk and recovery is so difficult to maintain.

Another reason why we were keen to write this book and use some of the analogies that we have in chapter four, relates to our experience of how the concept of self and self-image has changed in relation to the growth of the internet and social media. Social media and the internet have changed the world, how we behave, how we interact and how we represent ourselves has also changed. Social media websites and apps that are very image-led encourage young people to seek out perfection in relation to their appearance as these are the images that seem to be highly valued. Whilst this is unrealistic and potentially damaging, it also suggests that the way we look defines the way we are – if we look beautiful always, we are beautiful always and so there is no room for negative thoughts or expression of discomfort or distress. This creates the idea that you can only be valued if you behave or look a certain way. This may not always be in line with a young person's internal experience of the world and, as a result, they may develop psychological distress and symptoms that take the form of physical pain that can't always be reflected on. Our role as therapists is to support the young person to understand the physical pain as emotional suffering and to help them understand the meaning of it. Over time this becomes possible through the development of the therapeutic relationship. It is our privilege to be involved in these conversations and to support young people through these difficulties. We hope this workbook will inspire others to do the same.

Notes

1 Lindstedt, K., Neander, K., Kjellin, L. & Gustafsson, S.A. (2015). Being me and being us – adolescents' experiences of treatment for eating disorders. *Journal of Eating Disorders*, *3*(1), 9.
2 National Institute for Health and Care Excellence (2017). Eating disorders recognition and treatment NICE guideline (NG69). www.nice.org.uk/guidance/ng69.
3 Keski-Rahkonen, A., Raevuori, A. & Hoek, H.W. (2018). Epidemiology of eating disorders: an update. In *Annual Review of Eating Disorders* (pp. 66–76). CRC Press.
4 Curzio, O., Maestro, S., Rossi, G., Calderoni, S., Giombini, L., Scardigli, S., Ragione, L. D. & Muratori, F. (2018). Transdiagnostic vs. disorder-focused perspective in children and adolescents with eating disorders: Findings from a large multisite exploratory study. *European Psychiatry: The Journal of the Association of European Psychiatrists*, *49*, 81–93. https://doi.org/10.1016/j.eurpsy.2017.12.024.
5 Fairburn, C.G., Cooper, Z. & Shafran, R. (2008). Enhanced cognitive behavior therapy for eating disorders: The core protocol. In C.G. Fairburn (Ed.), *Cognitive behavior therapy and eating disorders* (pp. 47–193). The Guilford Press.

Chapter 2
Psychological distress and emotional experience in eating disorders

Overview	14
Understanding psychological distress	16
Basic human needs	16
Psychological distress	19
The development of psychological distress	20
Psychological distress in eating disorders	24
Experiencing psychological distress: deficit or resource?	26
The dandelion and orchid metaphor	28
The emotional journey from childhood to adolescence	33
The role of emotions	33
Childhood	34
Attunement and attachment	34
Gender	36
Food and communication	38
Adolescence	39
Parental relationships	39
Peers and identity	42
Adolescence and body image	43
Emotion difficulties in eating disorders	45
Emotions in the treatment of eating disorders	45
Eating disorder symptoms and dysfunctional emotional regulation	48
Helping young people to connect with their emotional experience	51

Overview

In chapter two there are three main sections. The first section introduces the idea of psychological distress and the concepts that are important in relation to human needs, such as social integration, individuation and differential sensitivity. We outline our view on how the failure to meet these two basic needs in a balanced way can lead to the onset of psychological distress. The description of the two basic human needs and the development of psychological distress are drawn by the Dialectical Psychology theory as defined by Ghezzani.[1] The Dialectical Psychology is a psychological and psychopathological theory centred on three fundamental concepts: needs, internal dynamic instances of the person driven towards their own fulfilment; alienation, a psychosocial condition in which the self, internally structured by social ideologies, meets their needs in a way that is incompatible with their own subjective limits and/or the human species as a whole; and the self-regulating function of the symptoms in relation to subjective alienation and the sociobiological disorder induced by it. In this work, the role of the genetic trait of sensitivity is also highlighted to help understand the person's experience of psychological suffering within their personality.

In eating disorders, the emphasis is on the need for individuation and differentiation. Young people are extremely sensitive to understanding the needs, expectations and values coming implicitly from their family and social context. They tend to prioritise them over their own in order to reinforce a sense of belonging. At the same time, they feel trapped in the relationship and find it difficult to trust the other, and would like to be more independent. The expression of their needs, the validation of their emotions and their individuation process, along with the need to differentiate from others, is delegated to the development of the eating disorder that for a while will represent for the person a form of identity, as well as express the conflict and the psychological distress generated by the imbalance described above. A theoretical model of identity, which helps to explain the impact of psychological distress on the development of identity is presented. Through discussion of this model, we introduce the idea of "filter" to describe the form of identity represented by the eating disorder. The introduction of the concept of differential sensitivity will help explain why some people tend to be more perceptive and attentive than others to the characteristics and the demands of the environment and have a richer internal emotional experience that will require longer to be expressed and understood. Within this discussion, we highlight the importance of the shift from the vulnerability/diathesis-stress model towards the environmental sensitivity meta-framework, which takes into account the interaction between both negative and positive environments and the specific characteristics and temperament of the person.

Understanding the emotional experience becomes important as a window towards the exploration of the subjective experience. It is understood that people suffering from eating disorders tend to suppress or misinterpret their own experiences of emotion and are overly reliant and sensitive to the feedback of others. It is suggested that eating disorders develop in the background of a vague and overwhelming emotional experience, as a way of managing emotions and as a way of regaining a sense of bodily self. This is the main theme explored in the second section that describes the biological, social and relational factors influencing the emotional experience through childhood and adolescence, such as gender, parental and peer relationships and body image. There are many areas of discussion that could be considered at this stage, however, we based our choices on the developmental contexts that we felt were most important in terms of our own clinical experience. The link between symptoms and emotions are introduced in the third section, which discusses the role of emotion in the development of eating disorders. We highlight how the emotional experiences begin with neurophysiological sensations in our body, which are then translated into thoughts and behaviours. We describe the reasons why young people with eating disorders find it so difficult to talk about their emotions. In fact, they often mistrust their own judgements or experience of emotion and become reliant upon the views of others to evaluate their own emotional experiences. In the same way that they tend to suppress their emotional experience, they also suppress and ignore the sense of hunger and fullness, which becomes an object of control. The whole subjective experience is alienated and emotions are channelled through repetitive thoughts and behaviours aimed at controlling the body and preventing the development of self.

We conclude that the main therapeutic goal should be to help the patient to explore their sense of self, starting from developing interest and curiosity to understand their emotional experience and how it reflects on their personal and social relationships. It is important to help young people to express their own needs and views within their relationships with the external context overcoming the conflict that they started against themselves and also against the others. We outline the framework of the therapeutic process by summarising its main steps, further described in chapter four, that can guide the therapist and the young person to develop a sense of ownership of their own experience and give a new meaning to their emotions.

Understanding psychological distress

Basic human needs

As human beings, we are consistently trying to get two basic needs met. The first is our need for social integration (the need

Psychological distress and emotional experience

to feel included in the world), which is met by forming close and meaningful relationships with others and holding in mind values passed down by family and social systems. The second need is that of individuation, which is the opposite, and refers to the need to feel individual and separate. This need is met by expressing our own qualities and pursuing our own goals. Throughout development, these two needs conflict with each other as individuals perpetually move from one position to another. In environments where the social integration need dominates, we may feel we are meeting the needs of others more and this can lead to personal suffering. On the other hand, when the individuation need dominates, we may experience a strong desire to fulfil our own potential, still mindful of losing the meaningful connection with others. The ability to balance both needs is important to sustain psychological balance, which is essential for psychological wellbeing.[1]

It is important that we understand the role of both these concepts. The need for social integration can be represented by both emotional and social bonds, often defined by the seeking

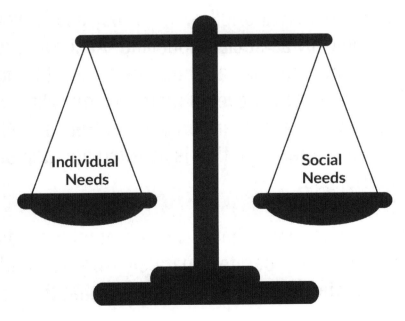

Figure 2.1 Two basic human needs

Psychological distress and emotional experience

out of warm relationships and social connections. Successful social integration can come at a cost to individuation, which can be defined as the search for distinct and autonomous personality. Individuation is often referred to as the separation of the child from the primary caregiver, however, it is more of a lifelong journey involving the relationship of the person and their social world and is best understood as a continuous process that shapes personality and identity.

Individuation represents a movement towards maturity and independence; however, social integration is key as it is impossible to find an individual position without understanding the wider world and views of others. To be completely successful at individuation would threaten psychological wellbeing as social withdrawal would result, creating further emotional vulnerability rather than strengthening the personality, which is the overall purpose.[2]

Human beings do not learn these concepts through direct teaching, but more through experience and awareness, which develop over time. Children watch the world around them and the adults in it and follow what they see, which is known psychologically as social modelling. According to their preference or desire, they pay attention to different things and through this process, they develop their own morality within each social environment they are present in. Hence, children develop their own moral code that is adapted and adjusted given their own experiences.

So, we begin to understand that these two human needs have their own identity. They operate separately from each other but, at the same time, they cooperate together so that the young

Psychological distress and emotional experience

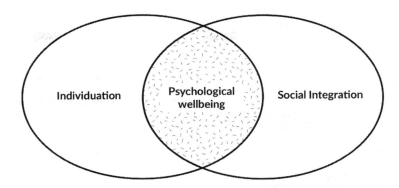

Figure 2.2 Psychological wellbeing: integration between social integration and individuation

person can develop psychologically. It is the integration of the two needs and the successful management of this through the different stages of life that will allow the young person to thrive psychologically. It is often when the integration is fraught with challenge and the balance is disrupted that psychological distress can manifest.[1]

Psychological distress

At times, these two needs can be in conflict with each other. At this point, if balance and integration can't be achieved psychological distress can develop. For example, a young person may be considering asserting their own personal needs, however, a conflict is created by the need for emotional belonging and social integration. The conflict arises between the need for dependence (social integration) and independence (individuation).[1]

In situations such as these, feelings like guilt, confusion, loss and separation and betrayal of loved persons and values may develop. The young person may be able to adapt to their environment but only at the cost of their own personal development, which can lead to psychological distress.

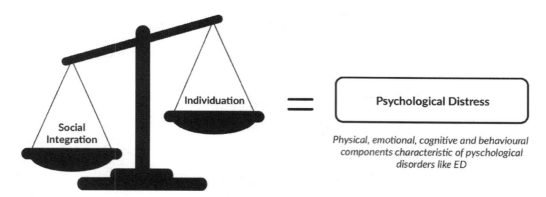

Figure 2.3 Psychological distress: imbalance between social integration and individuation

Here we use "psychological distress" to indicate all the physical, emotional, cognitive and behavioural components characteristic of psychological disorders and specifically of eating disorders.

The task of the therapist is to bring about a balance between individual feelings and social norms without, however, sacrificing the integrity of the individual. In other words, this could be described as helping build emotional awareness that enables the individual to manage the conflict without further damaging themselves or their social connectivity. Sometimes this task can be complicated as the psychological distress can be based in the dynamics of relationships that are highly valued by the individual and the society within which they live.[3] At the end of a piece of therapeutic work, the patient may have been changed through the development of self-awareness. The therapist will be changed too by the therapeutic process.

The development of psychological distress

There are both advantages and disadvantages to having two needs that need to be equally represented in our minds and personalities. The careful need to balance the two needs creates flexibility within the development of our identity, which lends

Psychological distress and emotional experience

itself well to allowing us to adapt to our social world and the characteristics we highly value. However, at times through the course of development, the personality can become unbalanced in one direction or another. Establishing and maintaining the balance becomes important so we can manage the continuous competing demands of dependence versus autonomy. Holding in mind the existence of these two basic needs, the development of identity goes through various different stages of discovery where social and individual needs interact with each other leading to integration and balance that allows the person to feel a sense of ownership over their own personality.

These ideas can be presented in the following way:

Identity I – Identity 2 – Identity 0 (Filter) – Identity 3[4]

With "Identity" here we mean all the processes that influence our way of being ourselves and being in the world. The "Identity One" represents the state influenced by social values. At some point Identity is impacted by certain emotional ties, social interactions or cultural values and is shaken by another intrinsic drive within the personality that would like to express its own personal needs – we call this "Identity Two". These two identities can be successfully integrated to form "Identity Three". This transition can be a long process whereby the person might experience a loss of deeply held values that helped them organise and balance their life. There may also be feelings of guilt and anguish when the person starts to focus more on their own personal needs. In this case, the person may feel stuck, and the need for individuation will be expressed through psychological distress and specific symptoms. This is the state that we call Identity Zero. It represents a sort of filter, a surrogate identity, that blocks the transition between Identity

Two and Identity Three but, at the same time, it represents the need for a change. In other psychological disorders like anxiety or mood disorders, the person in the phase of Identity Zero reports discomfort and experiences suffering accompanied by motivation to get better. The process will not be experienced as something easy or straightforward, but the person is motivated to change that state. Contrarily, the person suffering from an eating disorder feels protected by the symptoms and relies on them for a sense of confidence and a sense of identity.

The analogy of the filter becomes a very helpful way to understand this. A filter is a device designed to remove certain particles or block and reduce particular sound or light frequencies. The filter option is used all the time by young people in social media as a way to improve the image of themselves, to appear different, better, perfect before the eyes of others, but masking their more authentic and specific characteristics. This prevents the young person from engaging in a more direct and genuine relationship with others. The unrealistic idea of perfection seems to relate to an idea of self-sufficiency: "I'm happy, my life is perfect and I don't need anything else or anyone else. I am successful". In the filtered images there are no flaws, however, at the same time we may have the impression that that image is static and falsified, and we do not entirely believe in it. In fact, it is also an exterior image that does not mirror the internal experience of feeling vulnerable and not good enough, which are common in this group of young people. The filter is a symbol that represents a range of attitudes encouraged by the social system to present a coated image of ourselves, where emotions, vulnerabilities, pain, suffering, flaws, uncertainties are experienced as scandals to cover up. In the same way, the eating disorder symptoms initially give the young person a sense of safety, control and achievement. They present a filtered image of

Psychological distress and emotional experience

themselves, reporting that everything is going well in their lives, and they try to hide as much as possible their symptoms and their suffering, but also their own real needs and qualities.

We have chosen the filter analogy as it is a familiar concept to young people through their experience of social media. At times when talking about filters, young people will express a concern about meeting their peers in the real world, as they are worried that they will look different from the image they have previously presented. They often ask us what is the best way to create their own profile, and how much they can really say about themselves. They cite what is said about diets and body shapes in social media as if it were a truth, and the day after, they tell us that they need a social media detox because they can't think any more with their minds and they do not know who they are. They seem to constantly shift from absolute submissiveness to a total disengagement from the relationship. These difficulties, encountered by all young people at some point in their development, can take the form of a more serious conflict as expressed by the eating disorder symptoms. By using the filter analogy as the basis of some of the tasks presented in chapter four, we hope that young people will be able to start a reflective dialogue with us and understanding the meaning and impact of the eating disorder symptoms, which keep them distant from connecting with others and with themselves. One young person who was able to be very honest in therapy told us that expressing emotions to her friends made her feel vulnerable, weak and not understood, and from the time that she tried to hide herself and appear strong, she started focusing on food and exercise. These behaviours served as her filter. Only three years later, when the eating disorder symptoms were not concealable any longer and her physical health had visibly deteriorated, she sought help and started questioning the eating disorder filter. This was the start of her journey towards the development of what we call Identity Three. The task throughout Identity Zero is to resolve the psychological distress caused by the conflict between Identity One and Identity Two, the integration of their respective values in a new and original way will result in the formation of Identity Three.

Psychological distress in eating disorders

Eating disorders affect every age group, but for many young people, the adolescent crises and conflicts find a symptomatic manifestation in eating behaviours. Crises such as conflicts with parents, insecurities in social development and the search for autonomy can all be reflected in the refusal or excessive intake of food.

To understand the conflict between the two basic human needs in the development of eating disorders we need to ask ourselves two preliminary questions:

- What is food in the literal sense?
- What does food represent symbolically?

The human body has learned to distinguish edible from non-edible materials over the course of millions of years of evolution of the species. This very long learning has been memorised by human cultures and various cultural traditions have been undertaken to codify and transmit their food culture across generations.

This suggests that feeding a human being means accepting the importance of the food tradition, as it is passed down by every parent, family and society. Every child receives the food already chosen and prepared by his caregivers on the basis of trust. So, we can see how food is related to the need for social integration as it represents the first essential relationship of trust that every human being has with their family and with the society to which they belong. This allows the formation of what we called Identity One. As soon as the trust and the relationship are challenged by the need for individuation (Identity Two) the child can display disordered eating or eating disorders. Anorexic forms are a radical rejection of a profound belonging to a certain parent, family and society. It demonstrates that the need to differentiate is absolute, to such an extent that people suffering from anorexia nervosa can push their protest to death. It also represents the refusal of dependence, as expressed by the experience of weakness when "giving in" to the need for food, therefore implicitly to parent, family and society. The conflict is usually precocious and structured in fantasies of rebellion: the rejection of the primary relationship, the challenge to the environment and the fantasy of a total and omnipotent self-sufficiency from any kind of relationship and exchange with the world. Food is experienced as a stranger, an invader, a threatening element of the outside world that must be refused completely or swallowed and vomited before digestion, before it begins to be assimilated becoming part of the organism.

By refusing food the young person with anorexia nervosa engages in a powerful struggle against the parent or in any case against the family environment and the identity that this environment has transmitted to them. This opposition has the paradoxical function of defending the identity, the core of independence that has never really been achieved.

In order to preserve as much as autonomy as possible, the young person with anorexia nervosa denies or controls hunger, and while in this way they control their body, they have the illusion of managing themselves in their entirety. This is continually threatened by the incessant temptation of food (the return to the parent and to normality), the yielding to it, and finally, the repetition of the cycle. Therapy must move on two levels: a medical one, in which physical integrity is safeguarded – as much as possible in respect of the patient's wishes; a psychological one, in which the young person, who has never experienced it, is taught the difficult exercise of separation and autonomy towards the development of what we called Identity Three (see page 000).

This can be represented in a slightly different way in bulimia. In the bulimic form, this can be divided into two main types: oppositional and reparative. The opposition is a rebellion against the limitations experienced in the family. The reparative one is an act of compulsive appeasement of protest instances. Patients with bulimia nervosa tend to have more awareness, shame, remorse and guilt about their uncontrolled behaviour than those with anorexia nervosa and are more likely to admit their concerns. They are also less introverted and more prone to impulsive behaviours, substance and alcohol abuse and depression.[5]

Experiencing psychological distress: deficit or resource?

Until recently, most psychiatric research proposed one model of understanding psychological distress: the vulnerability/ diathesis-stress model. This model focuses on identifying risk factors, the most important of which was vulnerability. In this model, vulnerability was understood as a deficit of resistance or resilience, to the impact of negative environmental influences[6,7].

Psychological distress and emotional experience

According to the model, vulnerable children are more sensitive than others to adverse environmental conditions, such as the relationship with an abusive or negligent parent and traumatic events. On the contrary, others, more solid and resilient, in the presence of unfavourable environmental conditions are able to cushion the negative factors while remaining substantially intact. However, this model has now been questioned on the basis that it includes only a few variables, all of which are negative, and thus excludes any positive outcomes that those same vulnerable children have in favourable environmental conditions. Therefore, since the late 1990s, the research focus has looked at the development of vulnerable young people not only in negative contexts but also in positive ones. The research has tried to integrate the observation of positive developmental contexts, such as nurturing family environments and positive affirming experiences. It seems that a difficult individual temperament can be dependent on context both in a maladaptive sense, in relation to disadvantage, and an adaptive sense, in relation to advantage.

New research, therefore, includes positive developmental contexts and possible adaptive outcomes in their studies. As a result of these changes, terms such as biological sensitivity are becoming more suitable and comprehensive than the term vulnerability. New theories include Differential Susceptibility, Biological Sensitivity to Context, and Sensory Processing Sensitivity. All these models have been integrated to form the broader Environmental Sensitivity meta-framework. This framework provides a unique contribution to the study of individual differences in response to the environment. The framework agrees that individuals differ in sensitivity to environments and that only a minority of the population is highly sensitive, as though a minority is sensitive that this holds an evolutionary advantage. The research available on environmental sensitivity suggests that roughly 20% of the population is assumed to be highly sensitive and 80% less sensitive.

What was previously defined as a vulnerability factor, i.e. a difficult temperament, may in fact prove to be an important factor impacting positively on the child's development potential, if the environment changes. Recent studies show that difficult children are the greatest beneficiaries of a positive environment, for example, the experience of a sensitive and responsive parent. We know that, due to evolutionary motivation related to the survival of the species, people differ in the degree of sensitivity to the environment. Some are more sensitive to environmental influences, both in terms of increased adaptiveness in a positive developmental environment and also in terms of greater risk in an unfavourable environment. These individuals don't only benefit as much as possible from a positive context but are also more able to recognise and deal with any dangers more quickly.

The dandelion and orchid metaphor
This new theoretical vision can be better understood with the use of the dandelion and orchid metaphor[8]. Dandelions grow in uncultivated soils and do not require care to flourish. It is therefore a resilient flower. On the contrary, orchids, if placed in the same barren terrain, tend to wilt. According to the vulnerability/diathesis-stress model, we would call the orchid a "vulnerable plant". However, if the observation becomes broader by including what happens in a positive context, that is, an optimal terrain, something different emerges: dandelions do not benefit from a positive context more than they do from a barren terrain, whereas orchids flourish. The two plants are different, orchids, are more open to both positive and negative contexts. If we had observed only withered orchids would we have deduced

their adaptive inferiority with respect to dandelions? If we consider the comparison between the different developmental outcomes, we can understand that orchids are not inferior, or more vulnerable, they are only adapted to the right context, and in that context, they flourish.

Following on from this, Boyce and Ellis[8] talk about "orchid children": those children, with greater physiological reactivity, who, if placed in a positive context, have an optimal development and, if in a context that lacks nurture are more affected by the negative influences of the context. Dandelions reflect the majority of the population (around 80%) who are less sensitive to the influence of either positive or negative environments, whereas orchids (the remaining 20%) are more strongly affected by environmental challenges, but also flourish more in positive environments.

Alongside orchid and dandelion children there are also children even more surprising, highly open to only positive contexts and not overly influenced by negative contexts. This in itself is rather unexpected and needs to be explored in research. Only further studies, comparing different environmental models, will help us understand this.

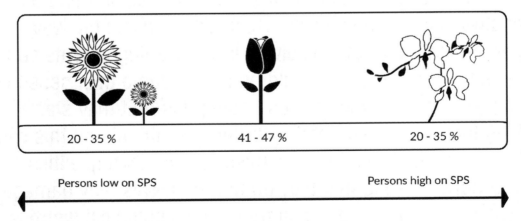

Figure 2.4 Sensory Processing Sensitivity (SPS) across the population[7]

Psychological distress and emotional experience

The expression "You are just too sensitive for your own good" is something we may all be familiar with. However, having a sensitive nervous system is normal, with sensitivity referring to the idea that some people have greater receptivity to stimulation than others. Stimulation in this sense refers to anything that wakes up the nervous system, gets its attention, makes the nerves fire off another round of the little electrical charges that they carry. So, people with greater sensitivity will be more aware of the subtleties in their surroundings, which is a great advantage in many situations. However, it also means that they are more easily overwhelmed when they have been out in a highly stimulating environment for too long, bombarded by sights and sounds until they are exhausted in a nervous-system sort of way. These differences occur because of the individual differences in the way the brain processes information. Some people are naturally more reflective, they sort things into finer distinctions. This greater awareness of subtle differences can make them more intuitive, which means picking up and working through information in a semiconscious or unconscious way. Furthermore, this deeper processing of subtle details causes them to consider the past or future more.

Therefore, being sensitive has both advantages and disadvantages. In our culture, however, possessing this trait is not always considered ideal, which also impacts the way the person feels about themselves. Well-meaning parents and teachers tend to try to help children to overcome their sensitivity as if it were a deficit. People possessing this trait may start thinking that there is something wrong with them, and this can lead them to adapt to others, dismissing their own qualities, or to withdraw feeling that they do not fit in. This may damage their own development and can trigger psychological distress.

Psychological distress and emotional experience

Alternatively, if the environment welcomes and helps them to understand and express their sensitivity it can be seen as a positive characteristic that can lead to emotional growth and development. People who are more sensitive may also possess some of the following abilities[9]:

- Better at spotting errors and avoiding making errors.
- Highly conscientious.
- Able to concentrate deeply.
- Especially good at tasks requiring vigilance, accuracy, speed and detection of minor differences (but not when watched, timed or evaluated).
- Able to process material to deeper levels.
- Often thinking about their own thinking.
- Able to learn without being aware they have learned.
- Deeply affected by other people's moods and emotions.

The above characteristics are further summarised by Elaine Aron[9] with the acronym DOES:

- D: depth of processing
- O: overstimulation
- E: emotional reactivity and empathy
- S: sensing the subtle

In summary, this new perspective had the immediate effect of increasing the number of studies that include positive factors, focusing not only on reducing existing problems but also on enhancing available resources. This promotes the idea that each individual is different from another and that a sensitive person needs special emotional and social coordinates for developing without damage and distress to fulfil their

Psychological distress and emotional experience

potential. Alongside this, we can also start to contemplate the idea that psychopathology can largely depend on insufficient consideration and inappropriate management of specific psychological qualities of which too little is still known.

Although more research is needed to understand the clinical applications of this perspective for young people with eating disorders, we wanted to introduce these ideas in the hope that it can be considered in the therapeutic work. Professionals who are working with young people with eating disorders might have noticed the DOES characteristics described (see p. 000) in almost each of the people they encountered in their services. We hear all the time parents telling us that their children think carefully about every single detail before making a decision, they are easily overstimulated and find it difficult to manage many things at the same time, they tend to have a strong level of responsibility towards others and they are like sponges absorbing the emotions of everyone in the room. This model helps us see our patients like gentle orchids, extremely attentive and sensitive to the implicit demands and expectations coming from the social system, possessing at the same time a deep reflective nature and rich emotional experience. These aspects make the interaction between the two needs more complex and it is important to support them to understand and express their own peculiar characteristics and resources. We hope that these characteristics if considered within the Environmental Sensitivity meta-framework will help us to better understand the neurobiological and psychological profile of young people with eating disorders and to help them to nurture their resources so that they can express their qualities, needs and resources in a healthy way, instead of channelling them through the eating disorder symptoms.

The emotional journey from childhood to adolescence

In this section, we are going to discuss the main factors across childhood and adolescence that contribute to the understanding of emotion identification, processing and expression[10].

The role of emotions

What do we mean when we use the term emotions? Emotions are important processes in our experience of life. They are neural and physiological responses to things happening in either our internal or external world, and they are also subject to a learning process based on what we are surrounded by socially and culturally. Emotions serve different functions; they impact our physical experiences and sensations and they also impact our behaviour and thought processes such as memory and decision-making capabilities. Emotions also help us to organise and direct our thoughts and behaviour and can be demonstrated through physical responses, thoughts and behaviours.

The first experience of emotion is when we feel something in our body, we will call this a physical response. This physical response triggers a thought or memory, which creates a mental representation of the experience through words, images, sounds or in other sensory ways such as smell, touch or taste. This cycle happens many times throughout childhood and slowly this will create our sense of self, which then guides us through our experiences of life. The way we develop our sense of self refers to the way we organise and integrate our range of personal experiences and different social interactions. This then forges the link between our own understanding of self-identity and our emotions. In other words, our experience of internal bodily

Psychological distress and emotional experience

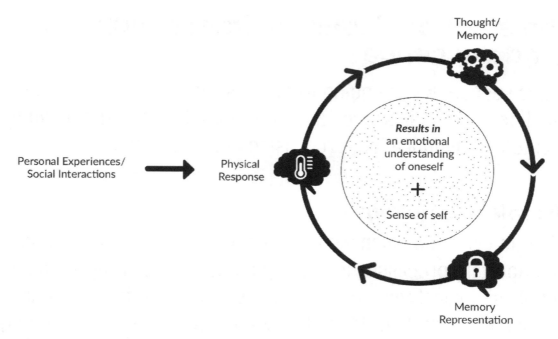

Figure 2.5 *The development of emotional experience*

sensations supports us to develop self-awareness and an emotional understanding of ourselves. One of the tasks of therapy is to gain some insight and understanding of how these two processes come together to form a personal experience of emotion.

Given the connection between individual emotional health and the understanding of self, it stands to reasons that when there is a disconnect between the two there could also be a detachment between feeling and behaviour resulting in a lack of orientation, or loss of direction and motivation leading to psychological distress.[2]

Childhood

Attunement and attachment

In early childhood, the relationship with the primary caregiver is key in containing the child's emotional experiences and to guide their future experience of emotion.

Psychological distress and emotional experience

There are two main factors that enable a good relationship with the caregiver and the resulting emotional experience for the child:

1) The capacity for the caregiver to hold the child's emotional and mental stages in mind and to reflect on it for the child.
2) The caregiver's responsiveness and ability to identify, model and name emotional experiences for the child, which is also called attunement.

These concepts are key in developing the capacity to identify the emotions of the self and of others and to integrate them into a felt emotional experience. This then forms the basis of a template for self and others in close relationships. This process is dependent on a "goodness-of-fit" between maternal and child temperament. When they are able to connect with each other, mutual regulation of interactions and communication of needs and attention are possible. When it becomes difficult for them to connect with each other's emotions and experiences, "mis-attunement" occurs and interferes with the development of the sense of self, which can relate to emotional regulation difficulties.

Also, eating disorders can be understood as a difficulty with attunement and individuation. This can lead to a sense of overwhelming emotional experience that cannot be fully integrated and is unable to develop into a coherent sense of self during adolescence. This results in poor understanding or perceived value in the individual's own needs and emotions, leading to reliance upon external sign reading and validation.

Psychological distress and emotional experience

Eating disorders emerge as a way of regulating and managing emotional experience while also providing a false sense of self and developing concrete means to meet those needs (e.g. weight and shape goals). The search for attunement leads the person to rely on external validation, which only serves to disrupt the expression of their own personal qualities and sense of autonomy, maintaining a negative cycle.

People who develop eating disorders struggle to validate themselves as separate and unique. As a result, they are left with a sense of their emotions and needs as being less important than those of others, or they may feel their needs should be suppressed. This results in poor emotional awareness and regulation, particularly in the context of attempts to please or meet the emotional needs of others.

Gender
There are many factors that help us to understand why there are gender differences in the way emotion is expressed, relating to biological factors, socialisation, social context and cultural expectations. It has long been suggested that gender socialisation and social construction of emotion expectations from childhood contribute to an increased risk of the development of eating disorders in women. It is proposed that parents socialise emotions based on gender, with girls being encouraged to internalise emotions such as sadness, fear, shame and guilt and discouraged to express anger, with the opposite being encouraged for boys. There is an expectation that girls will display a wider range of emotions than boys, yet may need more encouragement to learn to express their emotions than boys.

Girls also base their emotional relatedness on parental feelings, particularly the mother's, rather than their own emotion.

Psychological distress and emotional experience

Subsequently, women can find it difficult to define themselves without first contextualising 'self' within the mother-daughter relationship, leading girls to feel less powerful in parental relationships than boys. This can result in girls valuing interconnected social and emotional experiences more than males, and the cost of this is stunted development of their own unique emotional self-awareness and experience.

We know that eating disorders are more common in girls and women than in boys and men with a ratio of 1:8.[11] It has been suggested that this may relate to cultural ideals around the pursuit of thinness as desirable, however, it is also helpful to consider gender issues within this debate.

People with eating disorders report lower perceived individual autonomy and higher perceived cohesion in their relationship with their mother than unaffected sisters, although have similar perceived emotional connectedness. As a result, we expect girls to show more empathy and sympathy than boys, more sensitivity than boys to the responses of others (including both approval and rejection) and a greater need for approval superseding their search for autonomy. Together all these factors contribute to females considering their own subjective experience or evaluations as less valid than those of others. Indeed, it has been argued that mothers (consciously and unconsciously) direct their daughters in "gender appropriate ways" including offering the message their own needs and certain emotions are unacceptable.

In relation to eating disorders in young people, we tend to see low levels of emotional awareness, difficulties in identifying and describing their own feelings and limited expression of their own emotion and submissiveness, especially in

37

relation to conflict. Facial expression is often suppressed and emotional language is limited. Adolescents with disordered eating often devalue personal subjective experience and favour socially accepted and externally validated ideals (e.g. "thin ideal") as their own.

Food and communication

Feeding children is one of the most important caregiver tasks essential for wellbeing and survival. It can be time-consuming, tedious and exasperating. We know that for some children introducing new foods can be difficult with up to 15 exposures of the food needed in some cases before a food can be tasted. From a developmental perspective, this task gets harder around the age of two when children undergo a developmental shift, causing them to reject foods previously liked and accepted causing much frustration and confusion in caregivers.

It is of no surprise given the challenges associated with feeding children that emotions and mealtimes are strongly linked, and whilst this is largely a positive experience for most, sometimes negative emotions such as disgust and guilt can be experienced. Furthermore, adult food preferences are most likely linked to positive/negative experiences of food from an early age. Logic dictates that those with eating disorders have a greater link with the negative experiences of food for communication and emotional regulatory purposes such as rewarding, comforting or punishing. We know that even pre-verbal children can learn to associate food with feeling misunderstood, stressed and anxious.

People with eating disorders are more likely to have negative early life experiences with food and this in itself can be a risk factor. Once an eating disorder is present, caregivers become concerned and food becomes a method of communication. Food offers a way to communicate needs valued by the person with the eating disorder. This can serve as both a risk factor and a maintenance factor in the development of an eating disorder.

Adolescence

Adolescence is a challenging period emotionally and socially with consequences for emotion regulation and psychological adjustment. It is hoped that appropriate emotional development in childhood will provide the foundation for a child to build on in adolescence, with the development of a more sophisticated skillset such as emotion recognition, regulation and expression. These skills then become the tools that an adolescent can utilise to meet the social and emotional challenges of adolescence.

Other important tasks in adolescence involve the development of self-reflection and the formation of identity. Poor emotion awareness and a need to please others will create challenges at this stage. For some, an eating disorder becomes a way to improve oneself and to find validity in the expectations of others.

Parental relationships

Parents and wider social systems have an important role in supporting and promoting personal agency enabling the expression of identity and opinion without fear of rejection. At the same time, young people remain heavily dependent on parents, so it is an ever-changing balance of needs and adaptation for parents and adolescents.

During adolescence, it is important that parents can make their own shift, adapting and demonstrating flexibility in emotional responding. The purpose of encouraging emotional recognition in childhood is to encourage the child's labelling of emotion

Psychological distress and emotional experience

and support basic emotion knowledge and self-regulation. In adolescence the needs change; increased expression of reactive emotion or mirroring of emotion from the parent can increase the risk of emotion dysregulation and psychological distress. High levels of parental negative expressed emotion have been linked to the internalisation of negative feelings, which in turn can be related to invalidation of adolescents' emotional expression, and in turn, results in adolescents' emotional dysregulation.

However, as always, it is not an easy balance for parents to achieve as being overly dismissive of emotion can perpetuate the belief that emotions are dangerous or invalid and need to be suppressed.

The way that parents deal with emotion and their skill level in navigating the complex task of supporting an adolescent through this journey is key. Parents who are well socialised to emotions will find this easier. Parents who themselves have had difficult journeys throughout adolescent development may struggle and this can lead to poor parent emotional psychological outcomes for the adolescent in their care.

The stories that young people hear from and about their parents are also very important for the young person to develop a critical understanding of self. They can provide a powerful framework within which young people can then begin to understand their own experiences. This is referred to as the concept of "narrative identity". The development of narrative identity can also be influenced by gender differences. Mothers tend to support the adolescent child to construct narratives around emotion and vulnerability, using more emotion words and discussing the causes of emotion. Interestingly, both mothers and fathers use more emotion words when constructing narratives with preschool daughters than sons, focusing on the elaboration of emotions such as sadness and social-relational themes. The ability of children and parents to tell detailed stories about negative emotional events is related to adolescent wellbeing.

Subsequently, it is possible that there is less construction of emotional narratives and the development of narrative identity is impaired for those who develop eating disorders. We do know that adolescents with eating disorders have lower levels of self-differentiation, indicating high emotional reactivity, emotional cut-off and greater fusion with others, causing confusion between one's own emotional and mental states and those of others. They also describe emotional experiences with fewer words compared to healthy controls or people in recovery. They remember heavily detailed autobiographical memories and appear to struggle to integrate positive and negative emotional experiences, taking a very black and white view. All of these features may reflect poorer narrative identity within which emotions and emotional self cannot be embedded, further impacting difficulties in individuation.

In terms of eating disorders, parental separation can be problematic and may follow on from problematic interactions in early childhood. Young people with eating disorders have described their families as less communicative, flexible, cohesive and more disengaged, compared to young people where no eating disorder is present. Factors such as maternal criticism and emotional over-involvement are also linked to eating disorders. This would support the traditional view that families of people with eating disorders are enmeshed and rigid in their style.[12] This explains why working with families is essential in the treatment of young people suffering from eating disorders.

Family dynamics cannot cause eating disorders but they can act as a maintaining factor. Therefore, not only the young person but also parents can benefit from becoming more aware of how they identify, manage and express their emotions.

Peers and identity

We have all been adolescents at one time in our lives and we can probably remember the value of peer evaluation and the importance of social inclusion as opposed to exclusion. Gender differences and the intensity of role expectations become greater during this period. Sometimes there are difficulties in describing emotions, emotion acceptance and regulation, which, alongside suppression of own emotion and needs, may make an individual particularly vulnerable during adolescence when peer relationships and social acceptance become so vital. Adolescence is a time for learning a new way of being where the influence of peers becomes more important than the influence of family members or parents and this can impact on behaviours such as risk-taking and reasoning during adolescence.

Another factor that becomes very important in the process is social cognition. Social cognition refers to the mental processes underlying human social behaviour and interaction. This is important in creating a cognitive roadmap to support complex social interactions and decisions. In addition, brain changes accompany adolescent development and these result in increased capacity of metacognition – which simply put is the ability to reflect our own thoughts and behaviours. The capacity for this slowly emerges throughout adolescence. Not forgetting further neural and hormonal activity, which impacts social cognitive abilities, with attachment and mentalisation (identifying or inferring mental states of self and others) appearing to enter a continuous state of change.

Puberty is another key development stage, with social cognitive abilities such as facial emotion recognition and perspective-taking dipping due to hormonal changes. Subsequently, identity and other self-related processes become a source of information that can influence tasks such as decision making and intrinsic motivations. When a clear developing self is missing, extrinsic motivations such as the thin-ideal may become more powerful as the key driving force of decisions and behaviours. In eating disorders, weight and shape cognitions begin to emerge and drive behaviour.

Adolescence and body image

When we are born, we experience our body as something external to us, as evidenced by the surprised reaction that the child has at the sight of their own hands, of their own feet. The newborn treats the parts of their body as if they were external objects, and only after a long time with the help of the caregiver, these parts are integrated within a psychological experience. The identification with the body is therefore not given, but co-constructed, and the mental image of our body is built over the course of life starting from the very first days. We could say that the child sees themselves first of all in the mirror of the meaningful others. The relational framework of the relationships with the caregivers forms the basis of this process. Following on from this, the peer group, the first sentimental and sexual experiences and the social context with its cultural standards are integrated with each other to form the body image and satisfaction or dissatisfaction with one's appearance. Therefore, what we call body image is certainly not the faithful reproduction of our objective aspect. It is rather the result of a subjective interpretation through the integration of cognitive, emotional and social aspects. It is these aspects that need to be addressed and reflected on when we work with young people reporting body image concerns.

During adolescence when shape changes occur, some young people may perceive comments from others as external validation. The behaviour undertaken to reach this validation becomes reinforced, as does the pattern of overvaluing the importance of body shape and weight and the consequent behaviours that control them (e.g. calorie restrictions, vomiting, over-exercising). These become valued internally to support self-esteem and self-confidence, and externally to assure the experience of feeling socially accepted and liked. The psychological basis underlying the eating disorder is this omnipotent idea of controlling one's own body and emotions. This is reinforced by the real possibility, here and now, to do so and by the ethical social consensus shared by the global world. As we are all aware our social and cultural values convey the illusion that thinness is a guarantee of happiness and self-confidence. A recent example highlighting the impact that the social values and trends can have on the body image experience is the one related to the term "Snapchat Dysmorphia".[13] In early 2018, multiple newspaper outlets published several articles questioning the current impact of social media applications related to the choice of plastic surgeries. Some applications provide filters that allow users to change their skin tone, soften fine lines and wrinkles, alter the size of their eyes, lips and cheeks, and change various aspects of their physical appearance. They reported a case whereby a plastic surgeon was requested to make a patient exactly like one of her "filtered" pictures. Once again, we want to specify that social media do not cause eating disorders. However, at the same time, it is important to reflect on the always ongoing interaction between social and cultural values and the experience we form about ourselves from a psychological point of view.

In regard to young people with eating disorders, it is not that they perceive their bodies incorrectly, rather they have perfectly learned the dominant cultural standards relating to how to perceive them. The body becomes like a paper where they can write and communicate with the world, where they can redefine boundaries, where they can represent an idea of themselves and give meaning to profound suffering that they could not express in any other way. In fact, the self-harming behaviours directed to the body characteristic of eating disorders, unlike suicidal behaviours, have the function to maintain, through physical stimulation and pain, contact with life and the search for an identity.

Emotion difficulties in eating disorders

Emotions in the treatment of eating disorders

People suffering from eating disorders tend to suppress or misinterpret their own experiences of emotion and are overly reliant and sensitive to the feedback of others to assess if they are doing an adequate job. It is suggested that eating disorders develop in the background of a vague and overwhelming emotional experience, dismissive also of the physical response associated with emotions. Indeed, shape and weight concerns are thought to arise as the result of difficulty in experiencing one's own body (embodiment), influencing the development of personal identity.

Although emotion is complex, focusing on improving physical and emotional awareness in therapy will improve wellbeing as opposed to the over-reliance on the feedback of others to achieve emotional validation, emotional self-efficacy and self-agency. However, in eating disorders, this process is challenged by the value placed on the illness by the sufferer, which can lead to an increase in the lack of interoceptive and emotional experiences resulting in the disorder becoming a self-perpetuating cycle. Holding that in mind, the main therapeutic goal should be to help the patient to explore their sense of self, starting from developing interest and curiosity to understand their emotional experience and how it reflects on their individual, social and personal relationships.

For example, people suffering from anorexia nervosa have described the disorder as a means of forging a new identity, which becomes interlinked with, or replaces, the "true" self. Bruch[14] referred to anorexia nervosa as the "false self" that develops due to the sensitive self, struggling to acknowledge, validate and integrate the body and their personal experiences. This is how she describes the therapeutic task:

> *To help the anorexic patient in her search for autonomy and self-directed identity by evoking awareness of impulses, feelings and needs that originate within herself. The therapeutic focus needs to be on her failure in self-experience, on her defective tools and concepts for organizing and expressing needs, and on her bewilderment when dealing with others.*[14]

When we ask young people with eating disorders to talk about their emotions, we often get vague answers such as "Not sure" or "Hmm". It is difficult for them to engage in any conversation relating to emotion; their struggle with emotional processing and regulation are key features that underpin the eating disorder.

Psychological distress and emotional experience

This is easier to think about if we apply it to understanding symptoms. The symptoms of an eating disorder serve an important function whereby potential emotional expression is avoided by the development of predictable and controllable behavioural patterns. In terms of symptoms, we see a focus on food, eating, weight and shape, alongside thinking processes such as worry and obsessiveness. The physiological experience of feeling hungry or full is ignored and suppressed in an effort to gain control over bodily needs and further numb emotions. These thinking patterns provide an effective cognitive distraction from negative thoughts/emotions that become highly valued. These patterns also lead to a dysfunctional expression of distress and an ever-narrowing interpersonal life.

People suffering from an eating disorder often mistrust their own judgements or experience of emotion and become reliant upon the views of others to evaluate their own emotional experiences, which can lead to over-dependence on others. Being able to make sense of an emotional experience does not just help us understand our experience but also helps us to define ourselves. Therefore when this process is disrupted, it further damages the emotional sense of self.

The sense of self relies upon the personal experience of emotion (self-reflection) and feedback from others (external emotional validation). When there is a mismatch between the internal and external feedback, we tend to review our sense of self to minimise it. An internal mismatch can also occur when, during the review process, cues can be misread leading to inaccurate judgements about internal bodily states. Both scenarios lead to an experience of emotions as vague and overwhelming, and to inaccurate predictions relating to emotional information and thus a greater reliance on the feedback of others.

Understanding this process can also help us to understand the symptoms. For example, we know that "self-objectification", experiencing one's body through the eyes of an external observer, significantly predicts onset and maintenance of eating disorders over other more commonly proposed factors (e.g. dieting, body dissatisfaction). Continuous struggles in validating and naming the experience cause anxiety and a sense of uncertainty leading to unhelpful behaviours such as continual checking, worry/rumination processes, submissiveness and social reassurance seeking. The need for external reassurance further invalidates the internal emotional experience. Disrupted eating patterns can also result in an inability to update bodily memories, which goes some way to explaining the persistent belief in "fatness" or lack of insight into the physical severity of the disorder.

Eating disorder symptoms and dysfunctional emotional regulation

Emotion regulation strategies that allow for the avoidance of emotion can lead to the development of unhelpful over-regulation strategies. These over-regulation strategies can play a role in eating disorders as they become a way of controlling context and the potential avoidance of any emotion. Initially, these strategies may be perceived as useful as they reduce the intensity of emotions. However, they are maladaptive methods that will trigger further negative emotional experiences and reinforce negative beliefs. This in turn increases reliance upon the same maladaptive emotion regulation strategies, maintaining a vicious cycle.

People with eating disorders often struggle to express emotion but are able to suppress emotion and avoid conflict. Generally,

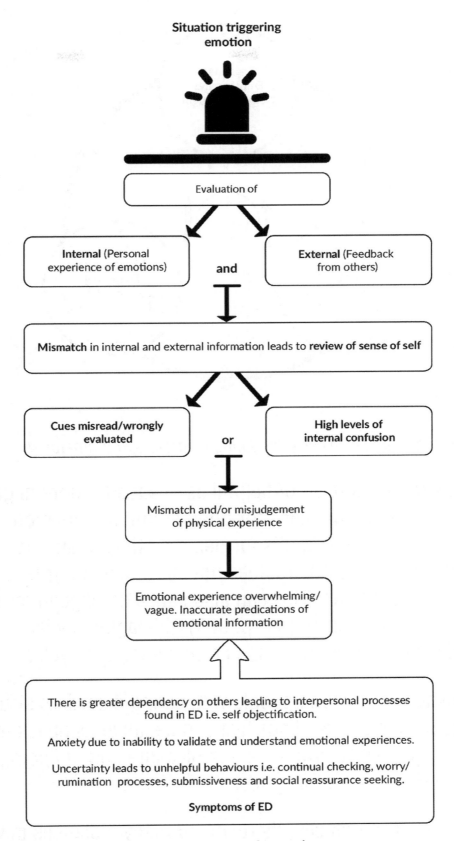

Figure 2.6 *Mismatch in the experience of emotions*

Psychological distress and emotional experience

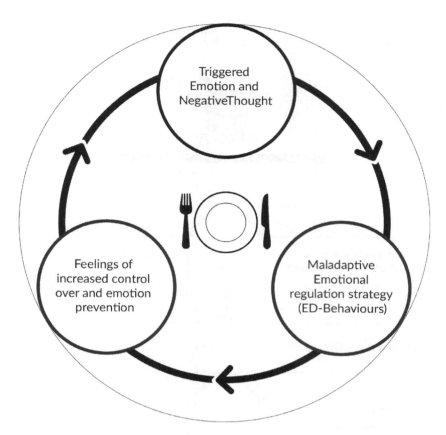

Figure 2.7 *Maintenance cycle for eating disorder symptomatology*

emotion suppression is not helpful as it leads to more negative feelings reinforcing the need for good emotion regulation strategies. To compound this further, the effort it takes to suppress emotion to others does not allow any congruent response to be offered. This can also cause damage in terms of attunement difficulties (see p. 000), damaging social connectiveness further and thus perpetuating the cycle.

We also know that young people with eating disorders struggle in distinguishing between positive and negative feedback, in experiencing positive emotions and pleasure and in finding words to describe what they feel.

Given our life experiences, there are so many instances in which the response you expected from someone can be misinterpreted and countless times when social interaction and connection can

Psychological distress and emotional experience

become further damaged. This increases negative emotional experiences, strengthens unhelpful cycles and thus an eating disorder can become embedded and helpful responses cannot be developed in a typical way.

Helping young people to connect with their emotional experience

We hope that what has been discussed so far has clarified the importance of helping young people to understand and connect with their emotional experience. As clinicians, we see this as an important task in the therapeutic work, which will support young people to overcome their eating disorder symptoms. The therapeutic work can be seen as a journey, and as a therapist you may be there for the whole journey or sometimes only parts of it. In chapter four, we have outlined which steps we feel are most important for providing guidance to the therapist for each step of the journey, based on the theoretical concepts described in this chapter. Here we would like to summarise them to create the setting for the therapeutic work, before proceeding with chapter three, which will give voice to the dialogue between young people, parents and professionals and the main themes discussed in the therapy room.

In chapter four we start the journey with the young person by eliciting curiosity about emotions in general, observing how other people tend to express their emotions and wondering about how they might feel in their day-to-day life. As this is the beginning of the work, we do not want them to feel overwhelmed by asking them about personal experiences and relationships, as this may be too intrusive. Young people often tend to idealise others and undermine themselves. So, we invite them to observe other people in their life and their idols (e.g. TV/social media stars, book characters) and become interested not only in what they express and present about themselves but also in what they might keep inside their internal bodily, emotional experience. This might help them to see others as normal human beings with their own vulnerabilities. It is hoped this might initiate the dialogue of helping them to reflect on social and personal needs and roles, and how we begin to integrate the parts of us that we present to others, with the ones we tend to keep only for ourselves as more personal. This relates directly to the concept of the two basic needs.

We would encourage them to think about what would our life be like if no one expressed their emotions, and therefore start reflecting on the valuable role of emotions. After a general introduction about emotions, the focus gently shifts to focus on their experience and their emotions, encouraging them to find words for what they feel.

The second stage aims to start drawing links between emotions and eating disorder symptoms. The focus is kept on the here and now and finding out more about their day-to-day life. Information about interests and activities will help ascertain information relating to behaviour around food and this helps us as therapists to understand what they value, what they like and what their characteristics and resources are, keeping in mind the orchid and dandelion metaphor. At this stage, it is also important to elicit awareness about eating disorder symptoms and how they impact on their routine. The discrepancies between what they show to others and what symptomatic behaviours they are trying to hide from other people are introduced and it is here that the concept of the eating disorder acting like a filter can be introduced and discussed.

Psychological distress and emotional experience

Once the young person feels more comfortable with talking about the eating disorder, the focus can be broadened to include not only the present moment but their story. We would help the young person to talk about themselves in general, paying attention to both challenging situations or periods of transitions, and pleasant moments and relationships where they felt more at ease with themselves and understood by others. It is important to encourage them to talk about their emotional experience with a special focus on their bodily sensation so that the body can become their ally, a compass to guide them, instead of an enemy to fight against and keep under control. We are interested in understanding when and in which situations they might have experienced a conflict between social needs and individual needs, and how they managed that conflict. Here we are interested to know about the development of psychological distress, with the framework described above, and how they get stuck in the Identity Zero/Filter state.

When the young person has a better understanding of their story timeline, and hopefully more awareness of how they tended to sacrifice their personal needs and views, expressing them with eating disorder symptoms, we would invite the young person to focus on the parts of them they feel are more personal and unique, that make them different from others. Here we would keep in mind the concepts of the individuation process and transition towards Identity Three.

Finally, we would support them to understand how to express and communicate these parts to their family and friends, to prioritise their own preferences and to respect their own characteristics and comfort zone instead of pushing themselves to adapt to the external demands with no acknowledgments of their own needs. This is based as well on the concept of Identity Three and integration between social and individual needs.

Each person would need a different amount of time to travel along each stage of the journey, and many times each stage would have to be visited more than one time.

For the purpose of the book, we tried to draw light on what we feel, based on our clinical experience, are the most important steps. Becoming ourselves, and overcoming symptoms that might hinder this journey, is not a linear but more a spiral-shaped process whereby we might have to revisit the same stages several times, but each time we can learn something more about our difficulties and ourselves. As therapists, we have the duty as well as the honour to offer guidance throughout the journey and the privilege to witness the blossoming of the self-development process in each young person.

Notes

1 Ghezzani, N. (2020). *La specie malata* (Italian Edition). Franco Angeli Edizioni. Kindle Edition.
2 Winnicott, D.W. (1990). *Home is where we start from: Essays by a psychoanalyst*. Penguin.
3 Watts, A. (2017). *Psychotherapy east and west*. New World Library.
4 Ghezzani, N. (2018). *Uscire dal panico. Ansia, fobie, attacchi di panico. Nuove strategie nella gestione e nella cura*. FrancoAngeli. Note: The description of the stages of discovery in the development of identity was introduced by Ghezzani. The concept of "Filter" and the description of its characteristic is an adaptation proposed by the authors specifically for the eating disorders.
5 Ghezzani, N. (2017). Disturbi alimentari. Un'analisi psicologica. http://nicolaghezzani.altervista.org/psicologia_disturbi_psicologici_ psicoterapia disturbi_alimentari.html. Consulted September 2020.

Psychological distress and emotional experience

6 Lionetti, F., Pluess, M. & Barone, L. (2014). Vulnerabilità, resilienza o differente permeabilità? Un confronto tra modelli per lo studio dell'interazione individuo ambiente. *Psicologia Clinica Dello Sviluppo, 18*(2), 163–182. Note: The concepts introduced in this paragraph are mainly based on this paper and the paper – see note vii Greven et al., 2019.

7 Greven, C.U., Lionetti, F., Booth, C., Aron, E.N., Fox, E., Schendan, H.E., Pluess, M., Bruining, H., Acevedo, B., Bijttebier, P. & Homberg, J. (2019). Sensory processing sensitivity in the context of environmental sensitivity: A critical review and development of research agenda. *Neuroscience & Biobehavioral Reviews, 98*, 287–305. Note: The concepts introduced in this paragraph are mainly based on this paper and the paper – see note vi Lionetti et al., 2014.

8 Boyce, W.T. & Ellis, B.J. (2005). Biological sensitivity to context: I. An evolutionary–developmental theory of the origins and functions of stress reactivity. *Development and Psychopathology, 17*(2), 271–301.

9 Aron, E.N. (2017). *The highly sensitive person.* Thorsons.

10 Oldershaw, A., Startup, H. & Lavender, T. (2019). Anorexia Nervosa and a lost emotional self: A psychological formulation of the development, maintenance, and treatment of Anorexia Nervosa. *Frontiers in Psychology, 10*, 219. Note: The description of emotional processing in adolescents with eating disorders is adapted mostly from this paper.

11 Steinhausen, H.C. & Jensen, C.M. (2015). Time trends in lifetime incidence rates of first-time diagnosed anorexia nervosa and bulimia nervosa across 16 years in a Danish nationwide psychiatric registry study. *International Journal of Eating Disorders, 48*(7), 845–850.

12 Minuchin, S., Rosman, B.L. & Baker, L. (1978). *Psychosomatic families: Anorexia Nervosa in context.* Harvard University Press.

13 Ramphul, K. & Mejias, S.G. (2018). Is "Snapchat Dysmorphia" a real issue? *Cureus, 10*(3).

14 Bruch, H. (1988). *Conversations with anorexics.* Jason Aronson.

Chapter 3
Therapy, clinical challenges and the world as a patient

Overview	58
On therapy	59
Understanding the emotional and social aspects of eating	59
The experience of therapy and the therapeutic alliance	62
The value of narratives	67
Challenges of working with young people with eating disorders	71
Family involvement	71
Weight preoccupation	75
The importance of body and mind connections in adolescence	79
Personality characteristics – perfectionism	82
Supportive language and feelings in therapists, young people and carers	87
Stages of recovery – dealing with anger and regression	87
Understanding the importance of therapists' feelings and sensitivity	90
Understanding the effect of praising in children	93
The world as a patient	96
The ideal child and the sensitive child	96
Psychotherapy of a pandemic	100
Understanding and promoting resilience	102
Pandemic and eating disorders	104
Rethinking mental health: ecopsychology	108

Overview

Previous research has revealed that many young people are not entirely satisfied with the treatment received and the contact experienced during treatment. Even people who experienced a positive outcome of treatment, as defined by clinically established criteria, describe that they have not been understood or that the therapist could not help them. In this chapter of the book, we focus on understanding the experience of therapy thinking about both positive and negative factors. The therapy process can be described as a mutual process whereby the therapist and patients co-construct the multiple meanings communicated by eating disorder symptoms.

The chapter has a section relating to the challenges of working with young people with eating disorders. This focuses on the importance of family involvement, the need to understand the positioning of the weight dilemma, the importance of understanding the mind and body connections and also the personality characteristics that can exacerbate them. There are many more challenges; however, we have focused on those based on our own clinical experiences of the illness and working with young people. Much of the content from this chapter has been drawn from aspects of our clinical experience and through the chapter, we have used clinical stories to share with our readers the value and importance of holding in mind these issues.

This chapter focuses also on the societal and cultural influences we and our patients are inevitably submitted to and how we can manage our relationships with the world differently to benefit our lives. The difficulties include those that the young people tell us about, how they see the problems and the world we bring into the therapy room with us. In relation to this, there is content on the recent pandemic, the impact of this on child and adolescent development and also the development of eating disorders. Finally, there is a section introducing the ideas of ecopsychology as a way of understanding the connection between our own personal world and the global picture from a biological and societal perspective. This also includes a discussion of the factors that will allow for more harmonious development, enabling us to cope and provide the best care also in difficult times like those of a global pandemic.

On therapy

Understanding the emotional and social aspects of eating

The way a young person eats can tell us so much more important information than just nutritional habits. It can tell us about how that young person lives, it can tell us about the structure of the family/world they live in and it can also inform us about the belief systems within that family/world. Eating then becomes not just part of nature but forms part of our culture. The preparation of food involves the transition from something natural to something cultural, and the way we cook food, the way we eat it and share it represent and reinforce the cultural values of both our families and the society we belong to. When we prepare food, the transition from a natural to a cultural phenomenon occurs.

Another important factor to discuss is the trust we place in those who feed us from birth. This trust is essential for our survival, but it is not absolute, and at times through our lives can be questioned and renewed impacting the quality of our relationships with our caregivers. American philosopher Robert

Therapy challenges and the world as a patient

Nozick[1] proposed that "eating is an intimate relationship", then when our use of food becomes distorted and an eating disorder develops, it is precisely this feeling that is lacking. When the relationship isn't functioning, food will lose all its relational, social and cultural qualities and become an obsession.

Regardless of eating disorder diagnosis, it is easy to understand if the young people we are working with have a problem by asking one single question:

"How much do you think about food during the day?"

For those who eat too little, for those who eat too much and for those whose food choices are absolutely dictated by their concerns about their health the answer is similar:

"All day long, I can't think of anything else".

Again, regardless of diagnosis, all eating disorders have the same obsession in common. The relationship with food takes the form of recurring thoughts that torment and leave no room for anything else. On a behavioural level, the obsession can look very different. Some young people will avoid food, relying on unrealistic self-sufficiency, convincing themselves they are undeserving of food and avoiding social experiences that may bring them into contact with food. Other young people may seem more in control, they may develop an expert understanding of nutrition, following a rigorously healthy diet. This is manageable some of the time but often they find themselves overindulging secretly in food that they have not allowed themselves all day. In all eating disorder scenarios, obsession and control not only take the place of interaction and relationships, they actually prohibit them.

Therapy challenges and the world as a patient

Food has several values in human life; it is our vital fuel that keeps us alive. It also represents the very first essential bond of trust that every human being makes with their family and with the society they belong to. For this reason, eating disorders seem to indicate the disruption of trust that every human being has with their loved ones. As discussed in chapter two, eating disorders express the sufferer's difficulty in regulating a balance between social integration and autonomy. Trust, created by the need for social integration, conflicts with a need for self-individuation that expresses itself through symptoms, rather than by developing an autonomous identity. By rejecting or controlling food, the person challenges the social bond and tries to look for their own identity. A symptom acts for a while as a surrogate of personal identity.

> *A young woman had become very unwell with anorexia nervosa; her weight was dangerously low. Her mother reflected on her own mistakes as a parent. She felt that the illness had separated them so much and whilst the mother was able to understand on some levels, she still struggled to accept this level of expression as it was so closely linked to suffering. She found herself in an apparently contradictory position whereby she felt that she had to connect deeply with the emotions expressed by her daughter's symptoms, decipher her extreme behaviours without being alarmed by them. As only in this way could she understand the message that her daughter was trying to communicate. This is a very tragic position for a parent; however, acceptance does not mean that the parent does not try to support and help.*

This example is important as it demonstrates the contradictory nature of the parenting relationship. On the one hand, the love is intense, and at the same time the love needs to allow the child to detach and separate for the child to become autonomous and independent. It is difficult to do both at once. These considerations are present in all relationships. The ability to recognise a person's right to live whilst fully recognising that "You don't have to be as I want you to be". On the contrary, "I will stand by your side and encourage you to become whoever you want". On the other hand, the other must be able to say, "I will stop trying at all costs to be as you want me to be". Only when we acknowledge the freedom of another person and stop attempting to control or avoid them can we begin to truly respect them and their needs. And only then will it be joyful and nurturing to sit together at the same table.[2]

The experience of therapy and the therapeutic alliance

Therapy has often been described as a journey. There are two people on the journey both the therapist and the patient. It is a mutual process, with mutuality being defined by the idea that two people are involved in the same process although it may be in a different way or to a different degree. Thus, the process is different for both the therapist and the patient, but it is shared and multiple meanings can be constructed. From this process a new meaning or view of the story of the patient can be thought about and shared, something that hadn't been thought about in this way before. The view of therapy described here is not consistent with the view of the therapist being the expert in the room, but rather it implies that both the therapist and patient are equals. At the same time, the therapist must have the capacity to contain the conflicts of the patient and to wait for the resolution to be found through the process rather than looking around for a cure.

Therapy challenges and the world as a patient

Within therapy for eating disorders, it is not helpful for there to be expectations on how the patient should respond to the therapeutic process as this would require a form of compliance to which young people with eating disorders are already very sensitive. The idea of the therapeutic setting is to create a potentially safe space wherein lies the chance for a young person to surprise themselves. It is this capacity to be surprised by oneself that allows a young person to step away from prior expectations and to move away from the expectation of compliance.[3]

The therapist's natural curiosity, which is key for the work, can help pursue difficult areas where the patient may be hurting. As therapists, we need to listen to the patients as they will allow us to explore these areas when they are ready. Nunn[4] proposes that we cannot make the patients and facts fit our theories and definitions of a disorder, but instead we should shape our understanding and theories around the patient's experience. In therapy terms cure means care. A therapist never offers a cure to patients but provides them with a model of care to support personal development, which can enable young people to find their true selves in a way that is acceptable to them. Winnicott[5] suggests that therapy is about guiding young people and their personal space, so that they are able to live creatively, involving something personal, perhaps secret, that is unmistakably themselves.

Research suggests that many young people receiving treatment for eating disorders do not view the treatment received as satisfactory. Even when outcome data can be positive, as defined by clinically established criteria, young people still report that they have not been understood in therapy or that the therapist could not help them. This is very important as we know that dissatisfaction with treatment has been linked to treatment delay, to the fact that treatment interventions have not had the desired outcome and to a premature ending of treatment.

As a consequence, these negative thoughts and feelings of depression or anxiety often remain in people who were dissatisfied with the ongoing treatment, something which reduces their ability to maintain normal weight after completion of treatment and increases the risk of relapse. Therefore, it becomes important to think about factors that can positively and negatively impact outcomes. Alongside clinical outcomes that form the basis of the NICE Guidance for treatment of eating disorders,[6] it is also very important to consider the direct feedback from the young people in terms of how they experience treatment and therapy.

When interviewed, the young people did not talk about the method or technique they found helpful, but instead, they emphasised the importance of the therapist's personal attributes.[7] They associate positive treatment experiences with therapists whom they regard as supportive and understanding, non-judgemental, warm, trustworthy, active, flexible, respectful, caring, validating and affectionate. Conversely, patients associate negative experiences with lack of validation, inflexible use of theory, treatment towards their person as an eating disorder patient rather than as an individual and the feeling of neglect and lack of care.[8]

Interestingly, young people do not talk much about what the therapist was like at the beginning of treatment, and when they do, they do it in relation to how the therapist's behaviour made them feel. Their story focuses on their own feelings and how the situation affected them. Young people commented on the

Therapy challenges and the world as a patient

importance of cooperation, balance, confidence and trust as important states for making progress in therapy. Engaging in treatment for eating disorders often means that for a period of time the young person needs to entrust others to make important decisions and determine how to proceed until they feel better and can control things themselves more effectively. For some young people, it feels good to hand over to the therapist, for instance, because they are unable to control everything when they are seriously ill, and for them, it is also important to gradually regain control.

At the start I was so unwell, that it was really hard to make decisions, I allowed an internal voice to make decisions for me. When I started to get better, I wanted to start making decisions myself again, this was a sign of feeling able to take control a little.

(Laura, 15 years)

Young people talked about wanting more information and wishing that professionals had been more open to alternative solutions. Sometimes they wanted to share this but didn't feel empowered to share their views on the treatment they were receiving. Some young people talked about needing to feel that each step of the treatment was designed for them and this provided a sense of ownership and responsibility.

As weeks passed, I was more able to decide what I wanted to talk about, how I wanted things to be. I was more able to decide these things, I was able to take responsibility. I understood that people around could help but I needed to take responsibility.

(Francis, 16 years)

Therapy challenges and the world as a patient

Most young people have one key professional who becomes an important support whilst in treatment, and the relationship with that person is often described as a complement to other significant relationships in the young person's life. The relationships in treatment became helpful when the young people met someone who they felt was just the right person for them.

> *One identifies oneself so much with the disease and one appreciates when other people do not do the same thing.*
>
> (*Vicky, 14 years*)

Young people with eating disorders are often very conflicted about starting treatment; this impacts engagement in treatment. It can take time, several sessions or more, for them to begin to open up. As in all human relationships, trust does not come about immediately, but can only emerge slowly if nurtured by consistent presence, care and honesty. When the patient allows us to see them when they suffer, there is the possibility of a trustworthy relationship – the so-called therapeutic alliance – starting to develop.

> *At the start I was unhappy and cross, I said I didn't want to go. I didn't answer anything, I sat in silence. As time went on, I was able to trust my therapist, our talking became more significant. I invited her into my world and started to trust her.*
>
> (*James, 17 years*)

The warmth and gentle tenacity of the therapist are key in the face of repeated resistance. The invitation must be kindly offered again and again until the young person realises that the therapist is there to help. The strength of the relationship between the

Therapy challenges and the world as a patient

young person and the therapist is of great importance to the treatment outcome. The therapist needs to skilfully weave into patient views on treatment and the two parties should be in agreement about common goals and the shape of the treatment. The therapist's qualities can impact on the alliance and person fit is never more important than in this instance. To confuse us further, young people have described important characteristics in a rather contradictory way, they value "kindness" but at the same time "firm", "professional" but at the same time "human". Whilst the therapist may have a wealth of experience, they view each young person's journey as a unique experience.

The value of narratives

In relation to physical and psychological health, we do not always know how long young people will remain ill or how long it will take them to recover. Regardless of our role as clinician, parent or carer, this is very hard to accept as all of us would prefer to know the exact course of the illness and when the resolution will be found. Even before we think about the course of the illness, we ask ourselves about the meaning. Our thoughts, feelings and stories around the illness and recovery journey can be termed as narratives. A narrative is another word for a story or an account of a series of related events or experiences. These stories can be true such as a memoir or autobiography or fictitious like a fairy tale or novel. Within this context, narrative psychology is a perspective concerned with the "storied nature of human conduct", that is, how human beings deal with experience by observing stories and listening to the stories of others. Throughout life we develop stories/narratives that can help us make sense of our experiences. There are several types of narratives that can be defined.

Therapy challenges and the world as a patient

The *restitution* narrative imagines a positive outcome, where illness is short-lived with improvements occurring soon, allowing the person to go back to their life exactly as it was before the illness. Another narrative is the *chaos* narrative, which imagines life never getting better again. In this case, the meaning of life has lost its internal coherence. The possibility of an illness is not contemplated as a part of life and it is experienced as a fracture impossible to amend. Alternatively, an illness can be seen also as the occasion of a journey that becomes a *quest* with the ill person holding a belief that something is to be gained from the experience.

These narratives shape experience, not only of patients but of clinicians as well. For example, a patient living to a *restitution* plot would likely pursue, be hopeful of and expect recovery, whilst clinicians view the illness as a *quest* and would motivate the patient and their carers to explore the meaning of a symptom beyond its superficial manifestation. The type of narrative we opt for determines our approach towards the treatment and the recovery. Usually, in our Western culture, we are presented with *restitution* stories and their promise of health restoration in contrast to *chaos* stories that make for uneasy listening. We would also need to interrogate ourselves and understand whether our personal narrative is influenced by a narrative proposed by social media and cultural beliefs.

It is also important to consider that the narrative can change throughout the course of the illness, and different family members can hold different narratives. For example, many young people initially feel pushed by others to change and get better, while for them there is no need to change. Even the idea of being healthy can be seen as something detrimental, that should not be pursued. This is the case for many people with eating disorders.

Therapy challenges and the world as a patient

At the beginning of the illness, being healthy again could mean for a person affected by eating disorders going back to the time when they may have felt empty and ordinary.

Parents on the other hand tend to have a completely different view. At first, they see it as unsolvable *chaos*. They cannot see a way out because they do not even understand why a person should worry so much about eating in the first place. Later, they tend to shift from the *chaos* to the *restitution* narrative: *if previously you were eating normally and were fine, we will help you to fix this, you will eat again in an appropriate way and everything will be fine as before.*

As clinicians too we should be aware of our own narrative and how it is influenced by both our personal values and also our clinical background. Many clinicians adopt a *quest* narrative where a psychological symptom is always a warning sign, which is intensely asking us to respond to our inner needs. The symptom has a literal meaning; however, it also has a more profound meaning, which needs to be read between the lines and understood within the cultural, historical, social and psychological context of the person affected by it. It is an attempt to find a new way of being in the world. The symptoms are warning us that there is a contradiction amongst some of our internal values; and they are not allowing us to continue to push ourselves towards the same direction chosen so far. They are encouraging us to review our own self.[9]

However, it is important to remember that the scientific community and evidence-based practice, which focus on the medical objective model of science, lead us to focus on the neural, biological and behavioural aspects of the disorder and the symptoms. Essentially, medical science asserts that there is a single truth out there (realism) and we can come to know that truth through the use of non-biased procedures (objectivism). The eating disorders research has been no exception to this rule, which for us has come at a cost to the complexity of understanding achieved thus far.[10] It is important to question whether this approach depicts the full complexity of the mind and existence and whether integrating the current model with more interpretative and existential approaches helps to understand the richness of the human subjective experience in a more effective way.

Narratives not only reflect the nature of the illness experience but also can be constitutive of it. When illness breaks our anticipated life paths, our narratives lose sense and shape and so meaning and identity can also be lost. Adapting to such trauma is a process of narrative reconstruction, whereby new stories are created to provide new sense to the illness. At this point, it becomes better understood that recovery is not just a reduction of symptoms. It is rather a journey of personal discovery, growth and the emergence of a new self. It can be a personal, unique process of changing personal attitudes, values, feelings, goals, skills and roles.

Recovery involves the development of new meaning and purpose in one's life as the person grows beyond the catastrophic effects of mental illness. It is also linked to the fact that the recovery does not always involve a return to a previous state.[11] Rather, it is a lifelong process that involves an indefinite number of steps in various life domains. As a result, many people view the process of recovery as something that almost defies definition. It is often described as more of an attitude, a way of life, a feeling, a vision or an experience than a return to health or any kind of clinical outcome per se. In addition to being unable to return to their lives prior to their illness, some people in recovery would not want to go back to their lives prior to their experiences of illness because that would in effect deny and/or negate gains they have made in the process. We could stress this even more: their previous life and self does not exist any longer. This last element speaks to the fact that recovery, in contrast to an absence of symptoms, relief from effects of illness, or remediation of difficulties, often involves growth and expansion of the whole person.

Challenges of working with young people with eating disorders

Family involvement

The psychological distress at the centre of each illness can be viewed as the same. What essentially is being expressed through weight and shape concerns is a search for identity, with the first question being: "Am I good enough?"

For most young people the message "Yes" will be received in different ways from the people who love them; all of the different responses encourage personal internal growth. As already discussed in chapter two, young people in treatment for an eating disorder are struggling with the balance between the need for social integration (dependence) and the search for identity (independence). As young people in treatment, they are encouraged to involve their family. The parental role in treatment is about helping the therapist understand the development of the disorder, identify supporting factors and highlight the main family dynamics. In many cases it is the parents who look for help first. Although the young people themselves may realise they need help, they may be too fearful of what treatment might look like to ask for themselves. The family provides the context for the disorder, yet it is the young people who are expected to do most of the work as individuals and recover "for their own sake", and they need to be able to talk about certain things without parental involvement.

> *I was so cross as I didn't want to go to the appointment, I didn't think I needed to go but I went to show my parents that there was nothing wrong, that I was right when I said I didn't need to go. But everyone disagreed with me.*
>
> (*Lucy, 17 years*)

The way that families are involved in treatment depends very much on the family dynamics. Many young people value the idea of individual therapy sessions in combination with family-based therapy sessions. Family-based therapy sessions involve the parents becoming co-therapists and challenging behaviours that have prior to therapy been accepted. In this way, the eating disorder affects the whole family. When the family has to support the young person in such a confronting way the impact on relationships can be significant. However, most young people report that parents' participation had a positive effect on the result of the treatment.

> *It was so important that my parents were there too, [...] as they needed to manage my eating and support me at home [...]. They (the therapists) asked my parents what they felt and what they thought and what they saw [...] and in that way we came closer to each other, I think. [...]. We could be open and honest about all that and we tried to carry this on when I went home. At the time, I thought it was annoying; it is only now, afterwards, that I see that it was important and that it helped me a lot.*
>
> (*Chris, 17 years*)

Many young people talk also about their siblings being more involved in treatment. On reflection, they realise that treatment and management of their disorder may have occupied a lot of space within the family. Some young people are also able to reflect on their eating disorder behaviours and how these may have impacted siblings too, such as dinner choices and conflict around mealtimes. The use of family therapy can be an important method to try and address these fractures that can become permanent if not discussed and worked through together. Many families emerge from this process with a greater awareness of their family strengths.

What professionals say to parents

It is very important that parents and carers have the right type of information and that they can understand as much as possible about the characteristics of their children's difficulties. It is very important that they see themselves as an essential ally in the prevention and treatment journey.

Professor Dianne Neumark-Sztainer[12] began collecting all of the pieces of the advice that parents had found helpful in supporting a child recovering from an eating disorder. This collection comes from different professionals across the world.

Recognise the power of denial. If you suspect eating disorders symptoms, get an objective health care professional involved as early as possible.

Take a good look at your own attitude and behaviours. Are you eating only low-fat foods? Are you afraid of your child gaining weight? You will need to deal with these concerns and make some changes.

Therapy challenges and the world as a patient

Don't get tied up in feelings of blame; look forward to what you can do now. Remember that no one person is responsible for the eating disorder, but everyone needs to take responsibility for helping the child to get better.

Be strong in enforcing the rules set by your health care team. Your child needs you to be a parent now more than ever.

Leave the eating disorder to the professionals. You take care of your child. Find things to do with your child that both of you enjoy doing and do them.

Work with the professionals. Talk with them about your concerns about the treatment plan, about your child's progress and about difficulties you are facing. Ask them what you can be doing to help your child.

Look for ways to communicate with your child at family meals, in the car and at any other opportunity.

Treatment can take a long time; stick with it.

Get support for yourself as a parent. Find a supportive group of parents whose children have similar problems.

Don't give up hope. Treatment can be very successful and your support will make a big difference.

Let your children know that you love them, even, or especially when they seem as though they don't want or need love. Do this with words, touching notes, acts of kindness and through giving your time.

Weight preoccupation

Professor Bryan Lask, one of the leading authorities on the clinical and research work on young people with eating disorders, reported this thoughtful quote at the beginning of one of his many academic papers:[13]

> *When you tell grown-ups that you have made a new friend, they never ask you any questions about essential matters. They never say to you, 'What does his voice sound like? What games does he love best? Does he collect butterflies?' Instead, they demand: 'How old is he? How many brothers has he? How much money does his father make? How much does he weigh?' Only from these figures do they think they have learned anything about him.[14]*

In this quote, Professor Lask highlights the extreme preoccupation that professionals place on weight as an indicator of our patients' wellbeing. In both outpatient and inpatient settings, as professionals, we monitor the patient's weight at least once a week. The multidisciplinary team will try to understand the ins and outs of why the young person has gained 200 grams instead of 800 grams, and if the weight gain trend is not consistent, professionals become very concerned about the outcome of the whole treatment. The more the patients remain at a specific weight and feel that they have a degree of control, the more we as professionals think that this will reinforce their eating disorder thoughts and behaviours. On the other hand, the more we encourage them to gain weight, the more they would feel anxious and they will try to manage their anxiety by continuing to control their weight.

Professionals' preoccupation with weight seems to reflect the social pressure on achievement and exponential growth. As

Therapy challenges and the world as a patient

a society we promote messages consistent with the idea that children have to learn, from a very young age, to grow up as quickly as possible and to achieve specific goals as quickly as possible.

> *For example, Sarah, 11 years old, who at the beginning of her secondary school wanted to earn as many credits as possible to show how good she was on her schoolwork. The more the credits, the lower the weight, unfortunately. Based on the counterintuitive type of thinking characteristic of the eating disorder, losing weight is an achievement as much as collecting good school grades.*

Clinicians appear to be obsessed by weight and target weights and researchers and diagnosticians use a specific weight for height ratio percentage (%WfH) or body mass index (BMI), below or above which a disorder is, or is not, deemed to exist. They highlight that this ironic tendency can be risky, as we, as clinicians, feed into the illness if we prioritise weight as a measure of illness severity and view weight restoration as the main aim of the treatment. That is not to say that we are oblivious to other indicators of ill-health or measures of outcome. Certainly, we acknowledge the specific eating disorder psychopathology, such as the morbid preoccupation with food, weight and shape, and other pathology, such as guilt and shame, and the comorbidity such as anxiety, mood disturbance, obsessional thinking and compulsive behaviour. Sometimes we acknowledge the other multi-system physical correlates such as osteopenia and osteoporosis, and impairments in cardiac, renal, reproductive, gastrointestinal and cerebral functioning. However, it is weight and targets that trump everything else. Any skilled patient can make her weight appear to be higher than it is. Most professionals will be familiar with the methods commonly used, such as water-loading, concealing heavy objects, pressing down on the scales, etc. Others are less obvious.

It is interesting to think about why we put such an extreme emphasis on weight and BMI, all too often at the cost of the therapeutic alliance and other more profound features of eating disorder pathologies such as disturbed eating, cognitions, emotions and behaviours and all the other physical correlates of self-starvation and purging. Patients do in fact frequently tell us that they have gained weight, as per our prescriptions, but are nevertheless still tormented by anorexic thoughts and feel very sad and anxious.

> *When I reached my target weight we met increasingly infrequently, and then we worked towards an end. It was hard, it was like now I was at target weight everything was okay again and I was swell. Inside I felt like saying 'I am still unwell, I am still struggling, and if you leave I will lose weight again'. I was really scared that I was not better even though everyone thought I was.*
>
> *(Mary, 15 years)*

Lask and Frampton list several reasons in detail for suggesting that such an emphasis is at best unhelpful and at worst counter-productive, as summarised below:

- Weight is difficult to measure accurately.
- Weight is difficult to determine with any certainty.
- Targets tend to be selected based on such constructs as population means for age, gender and height. This makes no allowance for the enormous individual variation, event within

one culture or racial group, in what constitutes a healthy weight or BMI.

- There is no correlation between target weight or BMI and reproductive maturity, arguably the biological essence of good physical health in young women.
- By setting a static target weight for adolescents we are failing to acknowledge that when the patient achieves this target she will, in effect, have lost weight compared to her expected weight gain for age over this time.
- Weight is all too easy to manipulate. Patients commonly want or need to convince others that they have gained weight.

Lask and Frampton invite us to heed the wise words of the Roman emperor-philosopher, Marcus Aurelius (AD 120–200), who stated "Do not value something you can measure, rather measure what you value", and they suggest what we should really do:

- Reduce the rigidity of our approach to these weighty matters.
- Reconsider this inappropriate emphasis on prioritising of weight and BMI.
- Acknowledge the futility of our need for an easily obtainable measure of progress.
- Find a healthier way of coping with our anxiety when the need is not fulfilled.
- Broaden our minds, so that there is a greater emphasis on the far more valid indicators of good health.

It is now widely understood that as professionals we should encourage ourselves, and our colleagues, to take into serious consideration these recommendations (see p. 000) in order to continue to improve treatments for our patients and to help them to overcome their struggles. Motivational approaches have been a major therapeutic development in this approach. To try to understand the patient's motivation and track this through the therapeutic work. As a result, we can then begin to think about how we can handle and integrate all the contradictory and paradoxical characteristics that the young person presents with, and, most of all, how we can provide a relationship which could benefit this person's personal psychological growth, not the one dictated by external, institutional targets.

The importance of body and mind connections in adolescence

> *Throughout the course of therapy, my feelings about my body changed so much, at times I hated it but I became more aware of this through the process of therapy. I experienced an internal pain and suffering which made me detach from others [...] my body and my mind were very disconnected. Therapy helped me reconnect them. I was able to work on self- acceptance, and then able to build a bridge between my body and my mind. I learnt to observe my body but also to value it. I saw myself as whole again and with my mind and body together rather than separate. Looking at myself in the mirror was not so traumatic anymore. I stopped judging myself for each contour I did not like. I gave myself the possibility of taking care of my body, helping it to be healthy and to allow it to carry out all the functions for which it has been given to me.*
>
> *(Rachel at the end of therapy, 16 years)*

This young person was diagnosed with bulimia nervosa when she was 14 years old. The body image concerns were the most persistent ones. It was impossible to address them from the outside by engaging in endless conversations about the size of each part of her body. They had to be addressed from the inside by helping her to understand that the experience of the body is the result of thoughts and emotions about ourselves and is influenced by our relationships as well as social and cultural values.

Several personality aspects are involved in the development of body image. The main one is self-esteem, which allows people to have a positive view of their own bodies. Conversely, low self-esteem increases a person's vulnerability, also in relation to their bodies. Another personality characteristic which has a marked effect on body image is that of perfectionism, which can drive people to set idealised, unattainable standards. The need for other people's approval can increase the urge to achieve unrealistic body models in any possible way.

For professionals working with young people, it is always impressive to see the quantity and diversity of individual and group rituals enacted on their bodies. They dress, paint, pierce, dress up and manipulate their body in many different ways. Their goal is to make it pleasant, beautiful and attractive. In some cases, they want to express something distinctive about their personality. In some others, they want to make clear that they belong to a certain group of people with their own specific rules and values. It also represents an ancient practice, mainly performed during rites of passage, but one which, in contemporary society seems to be performed ever-more intensely by adolescents.

Therapy challenges and the world as a patient

Adolescents also use their bodies to express their difficulties. They display extreme behaviour such excessive dieting, intense physical activity and self-harm. The tendency to look over and over again in the mirror, with the illusion to cancel details experienced as flaws, is symptomatic of a crisis of personal identity. It expresses the difficulty for adolescents to be loyal to themselves and to acknowledge their intrinsic value. Instead, the body becomes like an object detached from them and fragmented in different indistinct parts. It is like they do not feel they belong to themselves any more. In consequence, the attention paid to adolescents' own bodies can become an obsession, as they continue to look for an answer to their own internal conflict through fixing something external. In simple words, it would be like thinking that we are going to rebuild the carrier wall of our house by repainting it. The two things are simply not connected. Therefore, we need to take into consideration the difference between thinking about our own body in an abstract or obsessive way and being able to represent the body in our mind, in other words, to create a mental image of it. Simply thinking about it is sterile, while representing it in our mind means engaging in a personal process, whereby we develop a representation of our body as a whole and give it a relational, social, emotional and ethical meaning.

It is during adolescence that this demanding developmental task needs to be completed, so that the young person will be able to build a body mental image which integrates biological, cognitive, emotional and social aspects of the body. The therapeutic work allows the person to access the mental representations of their own bodies. In order to facilitate the mentalisation process, it is pivotal to promote the development of emotional intelligence, which includes improving awareness of the experience of our own body.

Therapy challenges and the world as a patient

Personality characteristics – perfectionism

Perfectionism is never chosen. Rather, it is a discipline based on internal slavery, a sense of inadequacy and lack of self-worth. It has two underpinning aspects; coercion to achieve excellent social and moral performance, and a form of opposition expressed by physical and psychological symptoms that seek to sabotage the sense of slavery. Our natural need for social integration, active from the earliest stages of our evolution, pressures us to internalise our environment's expectations and cultural values. In a person with strong social sensitivity, external collective and moral values are extremely powerful and can be internalised in an absolutist way, blocking the expression of the person's own needs.[15]

Robert had a bright, confident smile at the start of his first therapy session. He wanted help as he suffered from terrible gastritis for several years. This impacted on his eating and food choices. Robert wanted to study medicine. He viewed himself as knowledgeable in his area of illness yet his medications had not helped him. Robert also talked about being anxious, particularly about university. He knew that medicine would be intense and competitive that he was already thinking about the most effective way to finish it as quickly as possible. Apart from his gastritis, life was going well. Robert's father was a doctor, his mother an architect and his older sister was studying law.

At the end of the first session Robert added 'And I make to-do lists', in a slightly embarrassed way. He talked more about this at the start of the next session and it transpired that at times of anxiety Robert would make notes of everything he needed to do during the day: waking up, getting out of bed,

Therapy challenges and the world as a patient

taking a shower, getting dressed, saying 'Good morning' to his parents, having breakfast, leaving the house, taking transport to school and so on. All of this took time away from studying and working. He could no longer concentrate on his commitments and he was afraid he was trapped in this vicious cycle. Evenings were the hardest because he couldn't stop giving himself all these orders, and he had started asking his mum for help.

Robert seemed almost remote-controlled. But by who? It was as if an external authority was observing him at all times, driving him to choose each gesture and decision with extreme care and execute each in a measured manner. His identity as son, dedicated student and friend had to be impeccable against the perceived judgement of other people.

First among these was Robert's father, himself a doctor, at the end of a vibrant career. His father had worked very hard and saved the lives of many children. He expected his son to do the same, without hesitation or objection. Robert admired his father very much, but at the same time struggled to understand how he himself could become a good doctor within a system characterised by a rigid hierarchy, an environment where professors could not be challenged and where students were encouraged to compete against each other. Working hours, for the most part, were spent in mnemonic learning of all possible diseases and administrative practices, limiting time spent in human engagement and deep knowledge of patients. Robert could not express the conflict he felt, he wanted to learn to care for other people but the hospital seemed to him inhuman.

Therapy challenges and the world as a patient

Remember, in chapter two, the metaphor of orchids and dandelions. Robert's story is a good example of this. Robert could be likened to the orchid in this example whereby he can thrive but especially in external conditions that are able to provide optimal care and are respectful of his nature, otherwise he would suffer and sacrifice his needs while attempting to adjust to an environment he perceives as not belonging to him. His father instead could be likened to the dandelion, robust and that can grow anywhere, also in tougher conditions, because he is less sensitive to how external demands can impact the development and expression of his own qualities. The reasons for these differences in personality and temperament are not always immediately known or understood, but in relation to psychological functioning, it is important to have this understanding to enable different people to thrive in different conditions.

Whenever these feelings of doubt and agitation surfaced, Robert unknowingly suppressed them through rules and rituals, which not only controlled his day but his emotions. He had learned to do this when he was little, always behaving as a good and diligent child, and giving space to his sister who was very lively and needed a lot of attention. Not only that, whenever his industrious routine was interrupted by emotional experiences such as falling in love, teenage passions or anxieties, his family also required him to press on regardless of his studies and other duties.

Teachers had always rewarded Robert for his academic successes and professors continued to do the same at university. There was no room for his emotions, which over the years began to take the form of physical symptoms such as gastritis, intense anxious states and extremely controlled eating. Whenever he tried to explore his own needs and ideas, the ritual of making to-do lists, his way of showing himself and others that everything was under control, kept him in check.

Robert also controlled food. He loved to cook, but principally for other people's enjoyment. He organised delicious dinners, each time offering a different menu. And while he was happy to receive compliments from his family and friends, he was beginning to tire of feeding only them. He himself compulsively counted calories. Throughout his whole adolescence, he had maintained his weight at the lowest point in the 'normal' range. The needle on the scale had never moved a millimetre. A pound less and he would have been underweight, and his medical rigour would not allow that. An extra pound and he would have felt guilty for eating more than necessary. These signs, while not indicating anorexia nervosa as defined by diagnostic manuals, nevertheless flagged up a restrictive, anorexic attitude. Food for Robert served merely a survival purpose, stripped of the pleasures of personal gratification and shared partaking of meals.

Robert's attitude to food was the same as to himself. He didn't recognise himself as a person with emotional and relational needs, but rather designated himself as a kind of spokesperson for the codes of his family, university and social system. Robert's personality was organised around an obsessive perfectionism. His individual needs were stifled by fear of disappointment and not being accepted by others. His physical and psychological symptoms, and the frustration and malaise he felt, signalled to him that his ideal of moral perfection did not allow him to live his life, driving him instead only to meet family and social expectations. Robert felt great shame in asking for help because to do so invalidated his ideals of self-reliance and self-control. Fortunately, in therapy, he immediately recognised he could not submit to a behavioural regime whose rigidity denied him the nuances of his own emotional experience of the world.

Robert devoted himself to other people with a strong sense of duty, without ever allowing himself to submit to empathy and establish genuine interpersonal relationships. He lived a robotic life. The therapeutic process we embarked on together invited him to grasp the emotions implied by his symptoms: both those of anger and frustration at the performance demands from his family and university environment, and those of joyful enthusiasm for the medical career he wanted to achieve.

Over a period of time Robert was able to explore and establish a role for himself in his world, which allowed him to access his personal resources and sensitivities and have his own needs met. He was able to recognise and review his need to serve and please others. He realised that he could no longer solely operate with a mechanical efficiency to meet the demands of others; he needed to respond to his own internal needs and required genuine contact and personal involvement to feel fulfilled.

In terms of his physical symptoms and presentation, his weight remained stable over time. Robert learnt to make choices around his food based on his own preferences and desires. He was also more able to allow people around him to join him in food preparation and share this experience on a social level, relinquishing his need for control within this area of his life. His gastritis overall improved, however, when stress occurred he did experience mild symptoms. He learnt to view them as a warning sign and was able to step back and adjust his circumstances to ensure that the symptoms did not impact further. The body was something that no longer needed to be controlled; it became an ally that guided him through his emotional experience of life.

Supportive language and feelings in therapists, young people and carers

Stages of recovery – dealing with anger and regression

In this section we would like to introduce the stage of recovery model, something that Lask[16] discussed with both parents and young people as part of treatment. Both parents and young people reported finding this model very accessible as it seemed to represent their own experiences. As a result of this, we felt it would be helpful to discuss this model here and use it as a framework to help us understand the recovery process.

Given the complexity and severity of eating disorders in young people combined with resistance to change, the process of recovery is usually very slow. When working with young people with eating disorders it is important to hold in mind both issues relating to the pace and nature of change. At times, too much change can go hand in hand with what appears to be deterioration or, at the very least, patterns of behaviours that predominate at certain times. This can be demoralising for all involved in the care: the care team, the parents, the young person and of course the therapist. It is helpful to think of the process of recovery in stages. Stage One is that of the presenting problem when the eating disorder is the predominant feature. The young person tends to be preoccupied with weight and food intake almost to the exclusion of other considerations; at times schoolwork can be important but there is very limited interest in

Therapy challenges and the world as a patient

anything else. There is generally no recognition of the problem, but following the start of treatment, things can improve very slowly and these changes will continue, assuming the young person can tolerate the next stage.

Stage Two is often when a deterioration may seem apparent. In Stage Two of recovery, the young person can become increasingly assertive. They may feel consumed by powerful negative feelings, some of which may be directed to the parents but also clinicians. This is not characteristic behaviour for the young person and it can cause distress to parents. The young person is beginning to move away from trying to continually please and accommodate other people's needs. The young person starts to show anger and frustration sometimes for the first time. This can cause distress to parents who will be unfamiliar with a child who says no. This is a new experience for the family generally and can create strong feelings of paralysis within the family. This feeling can then be paralleled with feelings of deterioration as things don't generally feel any better. It is very common for a parent to feel angry with the therapist at this stage as things seem to feel worse. However, as therapists we are familiar with this step as a necessary step to recovery, so we not only predict this but we welcome it.

We advise the parents in advance along the following lines:

If your daughter is to make a full recovery, she will most likely go through a phase that you will probably find extremely difficult. This is a very trying phase indeed. She will be horrible to you and probably to us as well. You will be angry with us and feel that we have made her worse. However, we will be pleased because this will mean that she

Therapy challenges and the world as a patient

is getting better. It is as if she has been unable to express these feelings and they have built inside her almost to the point where she cannot eat. Once treatments start, however, these feelings will come pouring out like a volcano exploding. We will, of course, do our best to support you during this stage and it will come to an end. However, if you block her feelings, if you don't allow her to express them, or you punish her, she will withdraw and lock them inside again. You may feel better, but her eating problems won't resolve. Of course, you will need to set limits such as no breaking things or physical violence, but if you can tolerate the rest you will be helping her to recover.[17]

Stage Three is generally a calmer phase; difficult behaviours diminish and are replaced by a more age-appropriate expression of feelings. For example, the young person may express her anger directly at the person concerned, but within a few minutes is able to discuss it all in a relatively calm and rational manner. Once this behaviour predominates overeating problems and excessive negativism, Stage Three has been achieved and the child is well on the way to complete recovery.

Conceptualising recovery as a stage-like process can be very helpful but of course, it is never quite as simple as it seems here. There is often overlap between stages, which can last for a considerable period of time and sometimes there can be fluctuations. At times when there are traumatic experiences, such as abuse or violence, a young person can go through a stage of regression before entering Stage Two. This can be very difficult to manage and needs to be supported in a sympathetic and understanding way.

Therapy challenges and the world as a patient

Understanding the importance of therapists' feelings and sensitivity

Anyone who is going to see a patient tomorrow should, at some point, experience fear. In every consulting room, there ought to be two rather frightened people: the patient and the therapist. If they are not, one wonders why they are bothering to find out what everyone knows.[17]

Therapists are often asked whether therapy is effective. It is difficult to reply unequivocally to this question. Therapy is different in every case. When a therapist says that they adhere strictly to this or that method, some doubts arise about the therapeutic effect. We often hear patients saying that treatment is delivered at them, instead of feeling that they have the possibility to be involved and make a difference in their own treatment. The cure should grow naturally out of the patient themselves.

Psychotherapies are varied as are human beings and patients should be offered therapies as individually as possible because the solution of the problem is always an individual one. Universal rules are not possible. A solution which would be unhelpful for one person may be just the right one for someone else. Naturally, a therapist must be familiar with the different possible approaches and must take care to guard against theoretical assumptions. In dealing with individuals, only an individual understanding will do. Therapy is a dialogue demanding two partners. The therapist and patient sit facing one another, eye to eye; the therapist has something to say but so has the patient. In many cases in psychiatry and psychology, the patient who comes to us has a story that is not told, and which has a rule no one knows of. Therapy only begins after the investigation of the whole personal story. In therapy, the problem is always

Therapy challenges and the world as a patient

the whole person, never the symptoms alone. We must ask questions that challenge the whole personality. The psyche is distinctly more complicated and inaccessible than the body. It is not only a personal, but also a world problem, and the therapist has to deal with an entire world.

The therapist, however, must understand not only the patient; it is equally important that they should understand themselves and their own feelings as well. Only if the therapist knows how to cope with themself and their own problems will they be able to help the patient to do the same. When important matters are at stake, it makes all the difference whether the therapist sees themself as a part of the drama, or cloaks themself in their authority. For therapy to be effective, a close rapport is needed and that exists in a constant comparison and mutual understanding.[18]

The medical approach to psychological symptoms is leading us to forget the core of our work: being in the relationship with the person. The high-tech idealism is pervasive in our society. We need instead "high-touch" culture, services and relationships, and to use the "high-tech" not only as a substitute for ourselves but as an additional tool. This is also supported by the American Psychological Association, which prepared a Presidential Task Force on Evidence-Based Practice,[19] suggesting that central to clinical expertise is an interpersonal skill, which is manifested in forming a therapeutic relationship, encoding and decoding verbal and nonverbal responses, creating realistic but positive expectations and responding empathically to the patient's explicit and implicit experiences and concerns. They further note that research suggests that sensitivity and flexibility in the administration of therapeutic interventions produce better outcomes than the rigid application of principles. Sensitivity

Therapy challenges and the world as a patient

is defined as being susceptible to the attitudes, feelings, or circumstances of others; registering very slight differences or changes of emotion. It is also stressed the importance of a sensitive clinician's ability to learn to experience finer and finer distinctions or nuances. In many ways, this sensitivity is akin to a musical instrument, which must be carefully prepared, maintained, tuned and protected. And the therapy process is like an orchestra playing at a concert. Each instrument must be perfectly tuned and synchronised with each other. Every single element has to go into building the resulting harmony. The clinician's capacity for inter-subjective communication depends upon them being open to intuitive sensing of what is happening in the back of the patient's words and, often, the back of their conscious awareness.[19]

Sensitivity and emotional intelligence are key for both therapist and patient. A person often develops psychological symptoms because they are sensitive to implicit messages, emotional nuances and contradictions. They are able to understand what has not been said, to do what is expected even when they are not told.

> *Nicole, a 17-year-old girl, had been admitted as an inpatient. Nicole was very quiet and withdrawn, sitting always in the same corner of the lounge almost as if she wanted to not be seen by staff. Staff noticed that over a period of weeks she was the last one to be offered any psychological and nursing interventions and at times her peers did not invite her to join in with them. When spoken to, Nicole was abrupt in her responses. She had an unfortunate style of pointing out the mistakes of others. Consequently, the whole team tended involuntarily to leave her last as they felt irritated by her. Through reflective practice, the team reflected on*

their behaviours and feelings. They started to name feelings in conversations with Nicole and eventually, she told her therapist that when she was a child she was very reserved and immersed in her own world. Her peers did not know how to approach her and they did not invite her to play with them making her feeling excluded and not accepted. As a way of managing this difficult feeling, she started noticing all their flaws and criticising them, which reinforced the cycle of exclusion and irritation. As a group, the staff team was able to make the transition from self-preoccupation to self-awareness, which led to a greater awareness of the patient's experience too.

One of the major tasks in therapy is to be aware of our own feelings. They are very important. Feelings such as boredom, irritation or confusion experienced by therapists provide valuable information. If you have good self-awareness you can work out how much of these feelings belong to the patient and how much belong to you. It is important to be able to distinguish between the two because the patient who evokes the feeling in you may themselves be feeling that emotional state and they are bringing it to you in the therapy. So rather than feel discouraged by the feeling, welcome it into the therapy and try to use it.[20] Nicole was so dismayed by the possibility of being excluded and forgotten that her critical approach towards staff brought that very thing to pass. Nicole was able to recognise this through the process of therapy and realise that this was a pattern she had repeated many times and that she ultimately wanted to change.

Understanding the effect of praising in children
In the modern world, children and young people are continually praised, the belief being that this will impact positively on their

self-confidence and academic performance. However, praise does not hold the same meaning in the world of eating disorders and as professionals, we need to change the way we think about this. It was originally believed that people with eating disorders struggle to accept that praise was related to them, feeling like they did not deserve positive feedback and did not deserve to feel pleasant emotions. However, over the past decade, a number of studies on self-esteem have concluded that praising a child as "clever" may not help them at school, but rather could cause them to underperform. This will sound odd; however, studies found that children will sometimes quit when they have already completed the "best drawing". Alternatively, a child may simply repeat the same work: why draw something new, or in a new way, if the old way always gets applause?[21]

In a now-famous 1998 study of children aged ten and eleven, psychologists Carol Dweck and Claudia Mueller[22] asked 128 children to solve a series of mathematical problems. After completing the first set of simple exercises, the researchers gave each child just one sentence of praise. Some were praised for their intellect: 'you did really well, you are so clever'; others for their hard work: 'you did really well, you must have tried really hard'. Then the researchers had the children try a more challenging set of problems. The results were dramatic. The students who were praised for their effort showed a greater willingness to work out new approaches. They also showed more resilience and tended to attribute their failures to insufficient effort, not to lack of intelligence. The children who had been praised for their cleverness worried more about failure, tended to choose tasks that confirmed what they already knew and displayed less tenacity when the problems got harder. Ultimately, the thrill created by being told 'you are so clever' gave way to an increase in anxiety and a

*drop in self-esteem, motivation and performance. When asked
by the researchers to write to children in another school,
recounting their experience, some of the 'clever' children
lied, inflating their scores. In short, all it took to knock these
youngsters' confidence, to make them so unhappy was one
sentence of praise.*

If praise doesn't build a child's confidence, what does? It
doesn't make sense to praise a small child for doing what they
ought to be able to do. It is important to praise them when
they do something really difficult, like sharing a toy or showing
patience.[21] This idea can be applied to young people with
eating disorders. When, after struggling, they start to eat again
without adopting eating disorder behaviours such restriction,
bingeing or purging, parents, friends and professionals
automatically say to them: "Well done!" This then creates a
sense of guilt because they are still finding it difficult to nurture
themselves and acknowledge their needs, including the need for
eating. It also triggers a sense of shame because they know that
they are opposing themselves to the most natural process that is
eating.

To then praise the young person for doing this confirms the idea
that doing is more important than being, and that everything
can be transformed into an act of performance at which we
can succeed or fail. It would be more helpful enabling them to
observe and connect to the emotions and meanings they have
located in their eating behaviours. When they say "no" to food,
what are the emotions and experiences they are rejecting as
well? When they eat too much, what is the pain that they want
to push down together with food to the point where they stop
feeling the taste of what they are eating, but also of what they
are experiencing at that moment? When they purge, what are the

emotions that they are unable to digest, that have to get off their chest so forcefully?

In order to help them to develop their sense of worthiness so necessary for their autonomy, we have to be there with them, enabling them to witness their own internal experience. We need to be with the young person to let them know that they are worth thinking about. Without this presence, the young person may come to believe that their activity is just a means to gain praise rather than an end in itself.

The world as a patient

The ideal child and the sensitive child

In our current world childhood is a highly valued concept. Children are valued as they mark the transition from nature to culture, and they have to be integrated into the culture through caring and education. Through the child, a social group reproduces its way of being. Children are the future of every civilisation and if they are unable to confirm it, civilisation will eventually disappear. Our civilisation has now become fully aware that the survival of any social system depends on the socialisation process of childhood, hence the infinite attention to childhood psychology. The most specific effect of this attention to childhood was the creation of a new specific type of child, influenced by neoliberal socio-political values: the *ideal child*. The *ideal child*, as described by Ghezzani,[23] is intelligent and sociable, with skills suitable for competition to achieve wealth, prestige and to promote consumerism. Physical beauty, technical and intellectual talents devoid of moral values, extroversion as dictated by the TV stars and social media, superficial emotions not affected by the contradictions of the world and its social injustices: these are the main qualities of the *ideal child*. In light of this ideology, children who do not fall into the skilful and competitive model because they are different from others in that they are introverted, thoughtful, imaginative and emotional are perceived as ill and are, therefore, in need of an overload of attention and care. They are perceived as a problem and are gently pushed to correct themselves, to change their nature. However, in being sensitive individuals, they grasp the harsh aspect of this implicit social pressure and end up feeling ashamed and humiliated with an intense need for withdrawal.

At this point, this reaction is interpreted by adults as definitive proof of inadequacy or maladjustment, inducing further interventions. Finally, subject to a growing rehabilitation regime made up of parental anxieties, school tutoring and psychotherapy, the children end up giving in and are forced to model themselves according to societal needs, developing a false self and denying their individual characteristics. Children feel physically and morally defenceless, their personality is still too weak to protest, even if only mentally. The overbearing strength and authority of adults silence them, often taking away their ability to think. But this same fear, when it reaches its climax, automatically forces them to submit to the authority's will, to guess all their desires, to blindly obey them and to fully identify with them.

In addition, family, school and mass media oblige children to a tour de force in becoming adults as quickly as possible and they are removed from the spontaneity of childhood to be introduced into the ideology of scarcity and competition where they must work to establish themselves, grow, develop skills and enhance every aspect. Intellectual qualities have to be invested in school and social achievements, leading people to relate to one another

Therapy challenges and the world as a patient

according to values of superiority and inferiority. We can call this *anaesthetic code*,[23] which encourages extroversion, self-confidence and persuasive communication skills, a pragmatic approach to life to make use of social conditions in order to ensure personal success. Solidarity also becomes a constraint on social activism to be carried out with strength and determination. All of this is at the expense of empathy, understanding cooperation, interpersonal understanding and mirroring.

In children provided with critical thinking, sensitivity and reflective abilities, the *anaesthetic code* causes a strong feeling of inadequacy towards the social context and therefore a sense of shame and humiliation. Furthermore, if the child forces himself to conform, they feel guilty because they betray themselves. The child, not feeling welcomed and recognised for their individual characteristics, can come to attack themself and the social bond. The attack on the social bond is not, however, the expression of pure destructiveness to be limited and forced, but the expression of a search for individuation through developing personal autonomy. If this is the destiny to which the children of our society are condemned, it should be clear that the first truly ill person is not the child, but the world. Therefore, the children's psychopathology represents the failure of every society. Through their difficulties, the child tells us what the problem of society is. The response that the society offers to welcome individual differences is a determining factor in generating creative human wealth. If it does not welcome them, it condemns people to infinite repetition of copies of people all equal to themselves.

But what is the distinctive feature of children who suffer in our world? We can possibly identify it in sensitivity. In sensitive individuals, the ability to empathise with the other and to feel what the other feels resonates with intellectual aptitudes to imagine better emotional, symbolic and pragmatic realities than those in which we live. It is the tendency to inhibit rather than exhibit emotions and ideas, and process them subjectively and internally. They are gifted children with a strong sense of justice, beauty and harmony. Sensitivity is that primary quality of life that, by promoting identification with the other, prevents abuse and neglect. It is the attitude to use one's internal world to evaluate the world dynamics (critical thinking) and create a new system of values (creativity).[23]

The individual is always in intimate correlation with others and with the surrounding world. Therefore, the majority of evolutionary neurobiologists are convinced that understanding the other takes place precognitively. Even before our mind, it is our body that reacts to the emotion of others: our neurons, our cells, our hormones, our muscles, our bones, our hearts, our senses, our hair; everything in us is coordinated by the emotion that the other feels and by the thoughts that cross their mind, allowing us and forcing us to experience them. And so, we feel the others before any learning has taken place.[24]

Being critical and feeling the need to express one's originality and autonomy can cause an existential crisis. Young people, in order to develop their identity, must experience emotional and intellectual dissensions and divergences, and enter into conflict with the surrounding environment. It is, therefore, up to the human wealth of social systems and their moral tolerance to accept and integrate rather than reject and blame the manifestations of dissonance and conflict. The conflict with the world cannot be resolved in choosing between betraying oneself or others, but in adopting a dialectical approach integrating the differential characteristics of human beings and the complexity of their feelings. As human beings, we are animated by ambiguities and doubts. Conflicting emotions compete inside us in the same day and with the same person we can contradict ourselves several times. A child builds and then breaks a sandcastle; a boy loves his parents, but while talking with his girlfriend he speaks badly of them; one artist creates a cultural movement, then denies it and founds another; a man dreams of a career and pursues another; a woman marries a man while she is in love with another. Duality composes our life and structures our self.

Human beings have freedom that transcends historical-social conditions because they live on multiple levels of reality, and whereas society fails, they are predisposed to spontaneously generate solutions to their needs. Leading children towards therapeutic interventions, it therefore also means questioning ourselves and the world we live in, in order not to merely cure symptoms but to overcome the obstacles on which the symptoms were rooted and generate a new reality system able to allow for harmonious development.

Psychotherapy of a pandemic

It feels impossible to write this book and not discuss the most unexpected event that has overtaken the world in recent months, the outbreak of the COVID-19 virus, that quickly took the form of a global pandemic. As we will have all experienced, the world shut down and the death toll has been devastating. We are now starting to slowly recover but the future has never been more uncertain, and we know that we are not at the end of it yet, with second and third waves possible.

If we look back to history to learn, we know that the last pandemic SARS that crippled Hong Kong from March to June

Therapy challenges and the world as a patient

2003 produced secondary health effects that outlasted the pandemic itself. Depression, anxiety, PTSD, substance abuse, child abuse and domestic violence almost always surge after natural disasters and the pandemic is unlikely to be any different.

Whilst the coronavirus pandemic is every bit as much a disaster as any wildfire or flood, it is also very different from these disasters. Most people are generally resilient after disasters, with only a small percentage developing chronic conditions. Most disasters are specific to cities, regions or states. A global pandemic is different from this as there are no safe zones any more. A pandemic is an invisible threat; you can't see it or in some cases feel it. The world seems the same when you look but you know it is different. If we can't know where it is different it is hard to know when we feel safe. Such ambiguity could make it harder for people to be resilient.

Mental-health workers have never been trained in anything about this, and they are involved in the trauma as much as the patients and all the people seeking support. However, the core principles of disaster management remain the same: calming, self-efficacy, connectedness, hope and a sense of safety.

Furthermore, to avoid and contain the risk of catastrophic anguish present in all people who feel responsible for the destiny of loved ones, friends and those who depend on them, it is important to offer guidance towards lowering the level of strictly personal achievements. These personal aspirations actually coincide with requests that the social world proposes as ideal models, from which it is good to distance oneself to avoid further pressure, and towards cultivating the idea of shared responsibility and connectedness. Since no one can centralise the responsibility of collective destiny, it is good to dilute the anxieties and delegate part of their commitments to close people and to the social figures in charge, and to start immediate management of the psychological distress. As soon as symptoms of anxiety with catastrophic ideas develop, it is necessary to talk about it with a trusted professional.

Understanding and promoting resilience

It feels also impossible to talk about a pandemic without mentioning the need for resilience. Throughout the pandemic, resilience has almost become an overused word and it may well be helpful to clarify what is meant by it. It is not always easy to define resilience; however, broadly speaking resilience refers to someone's capacity to "bounce back" after experiencing adversity or challenging circumstances.

An individual's capacity for resilience comes from the interaction of many different parts of our lives that are connected. If we think about children and young people, it's easy to identify the different parts or systems in their lives that interact and will have a bearing on their resilience. There are many interacting systems such as peers, family, parents, school and community. So then resilience is dynamic. It can change across time, context and situation and individual resilience depends on resilience in other parts of the system.[25]

There is no doubt that the coronavirus pandemic has presented and will continue to present challenges for individuals, families, schools and local communities. Children and young people have been unable to attend school and see their friends or teachers. Some will have experienced sudden and upsetting events such as a family member being seriously ill, and some will have been bereaved. With this in mind, it becomes even more important to try and understand the difficult experiences that young people may have had. In this sense, resilience is not simply focusing on the positive and sweeping the negative away, it is about expanding our view of the negative to make sense of it, whilst also assimilating and allowing greater focus on what matters and what is needed to support a continued course towards a desired and meaningful outcome.

The factors that support the process of resilience for children have been discussed widely[26,27] and the most important factors include:

- A sense of belonging.
- Strong relationships.
- Agency.
- High expectations.
- The opportunity to participate as valued members of the community.

It would be easy for a child's narrative to become dominated by the language of risk, trauma, damage or illness. However, whilst it is important to not ignore the potential for trauma or harm it is also critical to create a space for a narrative that promotes and explores assets, strengths, hope and coping.

The pandemic has been a collective experience, and this in turn may promote a sense of belonging for children and young people. Many children have been able to connect with family members, friends or the local community in a number of ways during the lockdown period. The use of online video software, shared experiences like YouTube PE or seeing pictures of rainbows in their local community are but a few examples that have likely promoted a sense of belonging and connectedness.

On a very positive note, many families, young people and communities have reported positive experiences of personal resource and community support as well as facing significant challenges and distressing losses. Whilst it is important not to minimise distress it is just as important to recognise how much has been coped with, as we know that positive coping is associated with better mental health outcomes. Engaging with our coping, competence and resilience now is as important as preparing for the mental health challenges that may emerge.

Pandemic and eating disorders

At the stage of writing this book, the impact of the pandemic is yet to be fully evaluated. With that in mind, it is only possible to write about what some of the positive and negative impacts may be as data to support these assertions is not yet available. As we will have all experienced, the pandemic has disrupted normal life and it will take time for normal patterns of behaviour to return. New ways of being will develop as a result and some aspects of behaviour that were part of the pre-pandemic life will become redundant. This is an interesting time from a psychological perspective. We observed some dynamics specific to eating disorders during life in lockdown. The closing of society and the enforcement of lockdown conditions meant that young people's lives became smaller; more time was spent at home with family members and thus the need to be perceived a certain way in the outside world was removed for a time. This improved, for some, their experience of their body image and lowered the importance placed on school and sports achievements, as well

Therapy challenges and the world as a patient

as the pressure to attend social events with their peers. They told us that, almost for the first time, they were able to spend time at home without feeling they were disappointing someone, or they could read about the school subject they were really interested in. For others who may not have had access to the IT kit required to access remote schooling, it will have increased pressures. Also, people with strong anxiety and a need for achievement tend to live more in the future by planning always the next step ahead. In this case, they might have experienced more than others a sense of lack of meaning in their life, a sort of paralysis as they could not continue to work and plan at the same pace as before. This might have led them to place that need for achievement even more on controlling food, over-exercising and keeping busy schedules.

Spending time with the family caused as well both opportunities and challenges. Families had more time to talk and reflect on themselves and their difficulties, which might have inevitably led to discussions and arguments. Perhaps where family units did not function or cope so well, staying at home more may have been a struggle with the loss of valuable social connectiveness that may have served as a protective factor. Another common predicament was parents trying to encourage their children to push forward with their eating and recovery as "they had more time to focus on this", acknowledging soon after that the time was extremely challenging for everyone and they had admit their anxieties and vulnerabilities, allowing the space to share them with their children. On these occasions, pushing forward meant putting the illness of their children into perspective by seeing how the individual factors are always interconnected with the broader social elements and the recovery journey with the family instead of a solitary run towards some predetermined targets.

Therapy challenges and the world as a patient

Young people, more than ever, could see their parents struggling and in distress and became more able to accept their human imperfections.

We have also observed how young people have managed to spend more time on their own. Many of them admitted to us that they have overestimated the importance of social media and what they really valued and missed was being together with their peers. They were also able to review their values around friendships and important things in their life. Initially, they tried to keep a busy schedule and then gradually they felt more comfortable with a bit more boredom and tranquillity in their day-to-day life. For other young people, unfortunately, it was traumatic not having the possibility to access the physical presence of their teachers, friends and also therapists, so much so that they deteriorated to the point of requiring urgent inpatient admission. In a time like this, the sense of loneliness can make some feel more connected to other people knowing that they are feeling lonely too, but others experience an unbearable sense of alienation and sadness that may need immediate support.

Amongst these young people who struggled the most with mental health issues, some will have accessed help and some may not. The general trend already seems to be that even with young people accessing help, they took more time to access help than in normal circumstances. This in itself suggests poorer outcomes for mental health generally and for the treatment of eating disorders specifically.[28]

For some inpatients, these young people may not have been able to see family members regularly. Treatment programmes

Therapy challenges and the world as a patient

based on graded exposure tasks to food and eating may have been delayed so there may have been less practise time before discharge home to community teams. Others may have felt more pressure from parents to engage in therapeutic interventions to recover. Therapy may have been delivered face to face or it may have shifted to video conferencing, inducing a further sense of isolation and detachment for some.

In terms of young people receiving community interventions, only the physical aspects of their illness will have been monitored by healthcare professionals face to face. In most instances, therapy will have been delivered via video conferencing with some young people preferring this medium and others choosing to opt out completely. The threshold for risk assessment will have been greater for most young people with eating disorders and some young people displaying difficulties will not have accessed the care they needed when they needed it, again impacting negatively on the recovery trajectory.

We are grateful to all the young people that trusted us to support them throughout such a difficult time and invited us virtually into the private space of their bedrooms and living rooms. Online therapy allowed us to remain close to them and to continue our journey together. We were able to reflect with them on the essential characteristics behind the eating disorder symptoms that will lead them to thrive: a strong sense of responsibility and duty, intense drive towards self-sufficiency, as well as sensitivity to other people's needs. These are all resources, that when understood and not channelled rigidly into unhelpful behaviours, become fundamental to cope in times like this, and will allow them to be intelligent, respectful and creative members of society.

Rethinking mental health: ecopsychology

The coronavirus may also change the way we think about mental health more broadly. Perhaps, the prevalence of pandemic-related psychological conditions will have a destigmatising effect, as we can recognise in each other the same vulnerabilities, and consider each other part of the same system.

Human beings need special attention and care: space and resources to express their biological identity, psychological attention, empathic mirroring, attentive and respectful parents, adequate education and public health. The care of human beings implies respect for their sensitivity, attention to their talents and resources for the development of their potential. So, a humanity capable of exploiting, competing, envying and consuming cannot be promoted any longer. Diseases, both physical and psychological, arise from an ecological imbalance of the global and local system. Unrealistic ideals, performance anxiety and a sense of social shame generate pathological anxiety, anger and depression. Exploiting and competing economies and high population density generate unpredictable viruses.

Medical and psychological sciences will have to be ever more systemic and ecological and know how to relate the subjective micro-world to the macro-world of global society and the planetary ecosystem. In this sense, we refer to the concept of ecopsychology – as defined by Ghezzani[29] – a psychological approach that has as its focus observing the interconnections between the planet, the society and single individuals. The recovery of mental and physical health and also of the economy on a global scale will have to pass through these two fundamental values: respect for psychological resources and limitations by lowering the pressure of individualism and increasing shared responsibility and commitment, that if disrupted would generate symptoms of anxiety, depression, traumas and interpersonal conflicts of any sort; and respect for the natural ecosystem ruled by a pluri-millennial balance, which, if disrupted, would continue to cause viruses and various climatic upheavals and outbreaks. We should, therefore, realise that the human mind works like the planet; it is governed by the same homeostatic laws. As Ghezzani points out[29] the Other is not only the person next to us or our loved one, but also the eco-physiological system that has regulated the balance of life on the planet for billions of years. Sensitivity, prudence, compassion, balance and respect must be the watchwords of the future era.

Notes

1 Nozick, R. (1990). *Examined life: Philosophical meditations.* Simon & Schuster.
2 Giombini, L. (2020, February 13). The contradictory dynamics of eating. *The Psychologist.* https://thepsychologist.bps.org.uk/contradictory-dynamics-eating.
3 Phillips, A. (2007). *Winnicott.* Penguin UK.
4 Nunn, K. (2018). Mythical truths for clinical practice. *Journal of Paediatrics and Child Health, 54*(1), 96–97.
5 Winnicott, D.W. (1990). *Home is where we start from: Essays by a psychoanalyst.* Penguin.
6 National Institute for Health and Care Excellence (2017). Eating disorders recognition and treatment NICE guideline (NG69). www.nice.org.uk/guidance/ng69.
7 Lindstedt, K., Neander, K., Kjellin, L. & Gustafsson, S.A. (2015). Being me and being us – adolescents' experiences of treatment for eating disorders. *Journal of Eating Disorders, 3*(1), 9. Note: The young people's experiences described in this paragraph are based on this article and also on our clinical work.
8 Gulliksen, K.S., Espeset, E.M., Nordbø, R.H., Skårderud, F., Geller, J. & Holte, A. (2012). Preferred therapist characteristics in treatment of anorexia nervosa: The patient's perspective. *International Journal of Eating Disorders, 45*(8), 932–941.

Therapy challenges and the world as a patient

9 Papathomas, A., Smith, B. & Lavallee, D. (2015). Family experiences of living with an eating disorder: A narrative analysis. *Journal of Health Psychology, 20*(3), 313–325. Note: In this paper Papathomas defines the three different types of narratives reported in this paragraph: *restitution, chaos* and *quest.*

10 Papathomas, A., & Lavallee, D. (2012). Eating disorders in sport: A call for methodological diversity. *Revista de Psicología del Deporte, 21*(2), 387–392.

11 Davidson, L., O'Connell, M.J., Tondora, J., Lawless, M. & Evans, A.C. (2005). Recovery in serious mental illness: A new wine or just a new bottle*? Professional Psychology: Research and Practice, 36*(5), 480.

12 Neumark-Sztainer, D. (2005). *"I'm, like, SO fat!": Helping your teen make healthy choices about eating and exercise in a weight-obsessed world.* Guilford Press.

13 Lask, B. & Frampton, I. (2009). Anorexia nervosa – irony, misnomer and paradox. *European Eating Disorders Review: The Professional Journal of the Eating Disorders Association, 17*(3), 165–168.

14 Exupéry, S. (2000). *Le petit prince.* In Lask, B. & Frampton, I. (2009). Anorexia nervosa – irony, misnomer and paradox. *European Eating Disorders Review: The Professional Journal of the Eating Disorders Association, 17*(3), 165–168.

15 Ghezzani, N. (2018). *Uscire dal panico. Ansia, fobie, attacchi di panico. Nuove strategie nella gestione e nella cura.* FrancoAngeli.

16 Lask, B. & Bryant-Waugh, R. (2013). *Eating disorders in childhood and adolescence* (4th ed.). Routledge. Note: We reported the exact words used by Professor Lask when talking to parents, as cited in his book, p.192.

17 Bion (1990). In Aron, L. (2013). *A meeting of minds: Mutuality in psychoanalysis.* Routledge.

18 Jung, C.G. (1995). *Memories, Dreams, Reflections.* Fontana Press

19 Schore, J.R. & Schore, A.N. (2008). Modern attachment theory: The central role of affect regulation in development and treatment. *Clinical Social Work Journal, 36*(1), 9–20.

20 Yalom, I.D. (2010). *The gift of therapy: An open letter to a new generation of therapists and their patients.* London: Piatkus, Little Brown.

Therapy challenges and the world as a patient

21 Grosz, S. (2013). *The examined life: How we lose and find ourselves.* Random House.

22 Mueller, C.M. & Dweck, C.S. (1998). Praise for intelligence can undermine children's motivation and performance. *Journal of Personality and Social Psychology, 75*(1), 33. In Grosz, S. (2013). *The examined life: How we lose and find ourselves.* Random House.

23 Ghezzani, N. (2004). Crescere in un mondo malato: bambini e adolescenti in una società in crisi (Vol. 48). FrancoAngeli. Note: The concepts of the *ideal child* and the *anaesthetic code* were developed by Ghezzani and are extensively described in this book.

24 Pievani, T. (2014). *Evoluti e abbandonati.* Giulio Einaudi Editore. In Ghezzani, N. (2020). *La specie malata: Depressione, angoscia e senso della vita. Psicoterapia del terzo millennio.* FrancoAngeli.

25 Masten, A.S. (2015). Resilience in human development: Interdependent adaptive systems in theory and action. *Pathways to Resilience III: Beyond Nature vs. Nurture*, Dalhousie University, Halifax, Nova Scotia.

26 Eames, V., Shippen, C. & Sharp, H. (2016). The Team of Life: A narrative approach to building resilience in UK school children. *Educational and Child Psychology, 33*(2), 57–68.

27 Roffey, S. (2016). Building a case for whole-child, whole-school wellbeing in challenging contexts. *Educational & Child Psychology, 33*(2), 30–42.

28 Nicholls, D.E. & Yi, I. (2012). Early intervention in eating disorders: A parent group approach. *Early Intervention in Psychiatry, 6*(4), 357–367.

29 Ghezzani, N. (2020). *La specie malata: Depressione, angoscia e senso della vita. Psicoterapia del terzo millennio.* FrancoAngeli.

Chapter 4
Exploring the emotional experience in eating disorders: guiding principles and notes for therapists to work with young people

Overview	**115**
Section 1 – Starving emotions	**120**
Overview	*120*
Task 1.1: Identifying emotions	*122*
Task 1.2: Life without emotions	*124*
Task 1.3: Why do we need emotions?	*127*
Task 1.4: How do we recognise emotions?	*129*
Task 1.5: Expressing your emotions into words	*132*
Section 2 – The eating disorder filter	**137**
Overview	*137*
Task 2.1: Setting the scene of your eating disorder	*139*
Task 2.2: Behind the scenes	*142*
Task 2.3: Keeping up the performance	*144*
Task 2.4: The eating disorder magnifying glass	*147*
Task 2.5: Removing the eating disorder filter –	
a language for behaviour	*149*
Section 3 – Making your playlist	**156**
Overview	*156*
Task 3.1: Making your playlist	*159*
Task 3.2: Unexpected scenes	*161*
Task 3.3: Watching the highlights	*163*
Task 3.4: Different versions of your playlist	*165*
Task 3.5: Connecting to your playlist	*167*

Notes for therapists to work with young people

Section 4 – New playlist, new self   171
Overview   171
Task 4.1: Rebranding your playlist   172
Task 4.2: New content in your playlist   174
Task 4.3: How would other people hear your playlist?   176
Task 4.4: Sharing your playlist   178
Task 4.5: Presenting your own self   179

Section 5 – Breaking free from the eating disorder filter   183
Overview   183
Task 5.1: Emotional talk with your family   185
Task 5.2: Rebuilding connections with your peers   187
Task 5.3: Respect your comfort zone   189
Task 5.4: Future aspirations   190
Task 5.5: Private place   192

Notes for therapists to work with young people

Overview

The author Karen Blixen said:

All sorrows can be borne if you put them into a story or tell a story about them. But what if a person can't tell a story about his sorrows? What if his story tells him? Experience has taught me that our childhoods leave us stories like this – stories we never found a way to voice, because no one helped us to find the words. When we cannot find a way of telling our story, our story tells us – we dream these stories, we develop symptoms, or we find ourselves acting in ways we do not understand.[1]

We hope that chapter four enables the storytelling of the recovery process. Each time we tell our story we extract parts from our experience and add emotions and knowledge we have gained after the event. Observing and acknowledging what is happening in the present moment, suspending the judgement and only observing and describing what we see around us and our own behaviours allow us to establish a relationship with our own reality. Then, by eliciting memories on how events evolved we reconstruct the narrative of our experience. Memory is not about simply reproducing a past event but about using the past to recreate, in the present, something new.

Chapter four has a very different structure to the earlier chapters; it is very much the "story" of the book. By now, having read chapters one, two and three, we hope that there is some understanding of how difficulties in managing emotions and developing a sense of ownership of personal experiences and feelings can lead to the development of eating disorder difficulties. As you will have read there are several psychological models that explain the many challenges of the adolescent development phase and how and why adolescence can be a time fraught with so much emotional distress and difficulties. We hope too that you have some understanding of how psychological distress experienced in this way can manifest as eating disorder symptoms.

Chapter four focuses on how the eating disorder difficulties can be explored in the context of a safe therapeutic relationship with the overall aim of improving the young person's insight into their emotional experience of the world and how this is shaping their responses to emotional pain leading to symptoms of distress. We know that beginning therapy with young people with eating disorders can feel overwhelming and challenging. It is very difficult to focus on the emotional experience and their internal world when we see how they are putting their life at risk by continuously harming their body through restricting food, or eating too much, vomiting and over-exercising. Our instinctive reaction would be to make them stop those behaviours as quickly as possible, but this will be experienced by them as too intrusive and forceful leading, more often than not, to an exacerbation of symptoms. When we swim in a stormy sea and we are afraid of drowning, being able to remain calm is what will give us the strength to float and go back to the seashore. In the same way, it is taking the time to gently explore the emotions hidden behind the unhelpful behaviours that will help us to establish a dialogue with the young people.

Through this chapter, we would like to accompany therapists in initiating this therapeutic dialogue with young people. We would like to make therapists' experience less overwhelming by

Notes for therapists to work with young people

offering some guiding principles and notes for the sessions. We thought that this could be helpful in particular when working with those young people who are not feeling ready yet to get better, who may be at a pre-contemplation/contemplation stage of change,[2] or perhaps young people who find it difficult to engage in a dialogue with a therapist, or who may have had a therapy experience that they didn't think was helpful. It is also hoped that the tasks are helpful for professionals working in the field of eating disorders for the first time as the tasks are comprehensive and written in a step-by-step nature. They might also be valuable for key nurses or eating disorder practitioners who have been asked to conduct a short-term and focused piece of work and might value having a structure for their sessions.

The tasks aim to introduce the value of exploring the link between emotions and symptoms and to put the illness into the broader context of the young person's story, taking into account also the broader social context (social, family values; social media values; values represented by the characters they like). The tasks aim to support the young person to develop their capacity to reflect on the interaction between their internal world and the external world and to help them understand the need to balance external expectations and their own personal needs and qualities, as described in chapter two. The aim of this is to empower the young person to value their own view of themselves and the world and to feel able to counterbalance their tendency to please and accommodate the external needs/values/expectations, which reinforce their unrealistic idea of being self-sufficient (e.g. *I can succeed and make everyone proud of me, but I don't need them and their support*). Overall, the development of this self-awareness will promote the beginning of the individuation process.

Notes for therapists to work with young people

Chapter four has five sections: Starving emotions; The eating disorder filter; Making your playlist; New playlist, new self; Breaking free from the eating disorder filter. At the beginning of each section is a broad overview explaining the role and purpose of each task. This outlines what might be helpful to think about in terms of what a young person and therapist might want from each section; what they want to learn about themselves and what they want to learn about their difficulties. The overview serves as the first point on the roadmap to help the therapist decide whether they feel the young person they are working with is ready for the tasks that follow. At the end of each section, we tell you about Laura's story, a clinical example of how the tasks have been used in the therapeutic work with one of the young people we met in our clinical practice.

The sections have been designed in a way that they flow from one to another. That being said the order is not critical to the effective use of the task, rather it is a guide that can be adapted to take into account the needs of the young person and where they may be in their journey. Whilst it is not critical to work through the sections in order, neither is it critical to work through every section or every task. This in itself may create anxiety within the therapist and young person. It is more about trying to think about what works for whom on an individual basis and to consider the importance of pace and timing, which is key for making the work feel relevant and useful.

Each section of chapter four is further divided into different tasks. At the start of every task is a "Notes for the therapist" section. It is important that when planning the session, the therapist has time to read these notes as they help guide the

Notes for therapists to work with young people

therapist through the delivery of the task, firstly by explaining the aim and then by following this up with further information that might help the therapist explain the task to the young person. As most of the tasks are collaborative it provides information for the therapist in terms of what they might be able to share to support the young person on their journey. The collaborative nature of the task also provides a positive social modelling experience whereby the young person can engage with the therapist doing the task as well, so the emotional experience is truly shared.

Following the "Notes for the therapist" section, in each task is a text box outlining what we have referred to as "Guiding principles". The purpose of this is to provide a theoretical framework within which the task can be placed in relation to theories and concepts discussed in earlier chapters. Its purpose is to act as a reminder of what is guiding the task as well as a helpful aid for the therapist.

The next section of the task is the information to be shared with the young person. The narrative is written as if it's being shared with the young person. The task can be read to the young person or the sheet can be shared whilst reading together. Alternatively, the task can be paraphrased or adapted to best meet the needs of the young person. Each task is explained with the young person's needs in mind and the language used is appropriate to this. Of course, you may need to add additional information at times to clarify questions the young person may have but ideally, the task information presented here should meet those needs. Each task is followed by a picture that visually illustrates the task. Sometimes the graphic can be used as something to complete together and other times it is used as a way of visualising the task more to enable the young person to grasp the concept.

It is important to acknowledge that a story can't be measured; however, sometimes it is helpful to understand how the experience may be for the young person. In relation to this, we suggest the idea of writing a letter to try to capture their thoughts and feelings about the experience. This may be something that they can revisit at other times in their life. Letter writing is a well-established therapeutic tool and is something widely used in clinical practice to help people reflect on their experience and capture something that can be revisited at a later date.

Section 1 – Starving emotions

Overview

The first section is important for several reasons; it may be the start of the therapeutic work and relationship or it may be the first time that the young person and/or the therapist has worked in this way. It feels important that this "being the start" of something is acknowledged.

The aim of this section overall is to introduce the idea of emotions. There are five tasks: How do we identify emotions? What would life be like without emotions? What is the purpose of emotions in our life? How do we express emotions?

For many young people this may be the first time that emotion has been talked about in a therapeutic way. It is important to hold in mind that this is a new area of discussion and a new way of

Notes for therapists to work with young people

working so everything may seem unfamiliar to the young person, and acknowledging this is always helpful. This experience may feel strange, it may feel uncomfortable or it may even feel like you are both learning a new language for the first time, therefore, offering reassurance will help. The first task in the set focuses on talking about identifying emotions; simply naming feelings after watching a programme of the young person's choice. This moves on to then thinking about the programme without emotion and trying to compare and contrast the two situations. Both these tasks are done through the third person to create a safe space that is non-threatening. Tasks three, four and five then move onto discussion about the purpose of emotion in our lives. This task is key to setting the motivation position for the next two tasks. If we are able to engage the young person in understanding the value of emotion, it then becomes important to be able to recognise and express emotions, which are the final two tasks. Both these areas may be new for the young person, depending on what type of therapy they have had in the past, but even if they are familiar with these ideas, they may still find open discussion a new experience.

As this section draws to a close we would anticipate the young person and therapist to both recognise that something has started. Perhaps the start of a piece of work or maybe even the start of a relationship. In many ways it is important that the idea of "finishing" the tasks does not take over. It is a step-by-step process that evolves over time and sessions don't necessarily have to be planned around "working through tasks", rather the focus should be on the relationship with the tasks, as this is very helpful to discussion and reflection.

Notes for therapists to work with young people

Task 1.1: Identifying emotions
Notes for the therapist

This first task focuses on talking about identifying emotions in normal situations. It would be helpful to make a conversation about emotions as simple as possible. To do so, we would invite you to ask the young person to simply name feelings after watching a programme of their choice. It can be either a video or a series. We have referred to only a video, but whatever forum the young person feels most comfortable with can be used. Using the online video analogy previously described, asking the young person to choose a video or a series, and asking them to try to identify some of the emotions most relevant to the video or series will help the young person to start exploring their emotional world in a day-to-day setting. Giving the young person a choice on what material they feel is most relevant to their everyday life will empower them to engage in the exercise in a shared and collaborative way with you as their therapist. The choice they make is important as it will help to inform your view on what they value and how they see things; it tells you something important about them. It is also a way to introduce the importance of considering the ongoing interactions between the external and the internal world and to mediate between competing drives and needs.

This is a collaborative exercise where you as the therapist are invited to share your view on a choice. It also creates the opportunity to role model what you are asking the young person to do. Hopefully, this will enable the young person to engage in the activity and, at the same time, normalise the experience

122

Notes for therapists to work with young people

and build therapeutic rapport, which is an important task in an opening session.

Guiding principles

Psychoeducation about the function of emotions in our lives with a focus on other people:

- Eliciting curiosity about emotions in general
- Observing how other people tend to express their emotions
- Wondering about how they may feel in their day-to-day life

Task 1.1:

With this task, I would like you to think about an online video or series that you have watched recently that you enjoyed, something that held your attention and made you want to keep watching.

If possible are you able to share your choice, could we watch this together as part of the work we are doing?

Perhaps together we could think about your choice, we could talk about the reasons you chose this piece, what attracted you to this, given there are so many things to choose from, why this piece, what did you like about it, were there bits that you didn't like?

Together perhaps we could think about the feelings that it created in you. I could think about the same and we could share and discuss this together.

Notes for therapists to work with young people

Task 1.2: Life without emotions
Notes for the therapist

Following on from task one, we would like you as the therapist to encourage the young person to hold in mind the online video or series they chose. Whereas in the last task you discussed in openly and collaboratively the emotion expressed in the piece, this time we want you to imagine the video with the emotion missing. To support the young person to engage with this exercise, it will be important for you as the therapist to do it first and model to the young person. Focus on a small section of the video, or one particular character or storyline, and talk with the young person about what you think this would be like with emotion missing. This part of the task is very important as it will enable the young person to engage more. By doing this as a task we are attempting to normalise emotional expression,

Notes for therapists to work with young people

both positive and negative, without thinking about anything too personal or emotive. This may be a completely new experience for the young person; past experiences might have led them to believe that talking about emotions is very painful and exposing. However, this task aims to help them to understand that emotions are a normal part of everyday life and talking about them openly can be a safe experience. It also introduces the idea of emotions as a very useful guide that helps us to understand what we need in a specific moment, what we like and to make choices about things we want to do and people we want to be with. This could enable the young person to start challenging the idea that emotions are confusing and a sign of weakness. By doing this collaboratively you are sharing the experience of talking about emotions and creating a shared common ground between you, which will strengthen the therapeutic relationship.

Guiding principles

Psychoeducation on the function of emotions:

- Playing with the young person, eliciting thoughts about life without emotions
- Working through alternative perspectives rather than doing this on their own
- Considering the physiological responses and interpersonal impact of emotions

---

Task 1.2:
Holding in mind the video or series you chose in the first task, try to think about this video or series with emotion missing. You might want to think about a specific scene or a specific character.

Notes for therapists to work with young people

I will give you a few moments to think about this. I am very happy to share my view first.

- What do you think it would be like?
- What differences would you notice in the episode or show?
- Do you think it feels better with or without emotions as part of it?
- Do you think you would have chosen it without emotions?

I wonder if we share any common ground with our thoughts regarding this. Perhaps we can share and discuss this together.

Notes for therapists to work with young people

Task 1.3: Why do we need emotions?
Notes for the therapist

The purpose of this task is to support the young person to distinguish between their internal and external world and to help them understand that there might be emotions that they are feeling that they do not show to people around them. The task also aims to help them understand and recognise that there may be inhibiting factors in terms of what they feel comfortable showing to others such as social factors, values and judgements. In the task you are asked to help the young person think about the main character in their video and to try to imagine what that character might be feeling. You are asked to think with the young person about what the character might be happy to share and what they might not feel comfortable sharing, based on what they think is socially acceptable and acceptable for them individually. You can discuss with the young person what we feel is socially acceptable. For example, you could think with them whether and when the expression of our emotions is influenced by social and family values. Often, we hear young people say that in their family no one talks about their emotions, or contrarily that one family member tends to be very expressive and anxious so that the young people prefer avoiding expressing their own to keep the peace. Other times, they recall having been criticised when they cried or were too excitable, so then they tried to over-regulate their expression. The cultural background is another important factor that can be included in the discussion as we know that different cultures promote a different degree of internalisation or externalisation of emotions.

Notes for therapists to work with young people

> **Guiding principles**
>
> Introduction of the concept of acceptable emotional expression and the need to balance social and individual needs:
>
> - Understanding of the individuation and socialisation process
> - Conflict and mediation between these two needs

Task 1.3:

I am going to ask you to think about the video that we have been talking about. I would like you to choose one character from the video and think about how they might be feeling on the inside and what they might show on the outside.

- Do you think there would be differences?
- Are you able to think about the things that they might not want other people to see?
- Are you able to think about why that might be?
- Are you able to think about any social rules or expectations that might influence the character?

Notes for therapists to work with young people

Task 1.4: How do we recognise emotions?
Notes for the therapist

The purpose of this task is to help the young person to engage with the main character of their video on different levels. The task asks the young person to observe the main character and to focus on how they present themselves in the video. It would be helpful for the young person to think about this on both a behavioural and emotional level if they are able to. To begin with it may be helpful to start observing behaviours such as non-verbal communications and how they match or conflict with verbal communications. Once the young person is able to engage with this part of the task it is worth trying to progress the task on to helping the young person to engage with how the main character may be feeling. This may be congruent or incongruent with the way they present and both scenarios are worth exploring as they will help the young person gain access into the idea of emotions and how they can be presented or disguised. This is to introduce the idea that, at times, we tend to keep inside what we feel but our internal bodily experience must not be completely ignored, judged or misinterpreted. For example, often we hear young people saying that they felt extremely anxious and agitated the day before a school exam and misinterpreted it as a sign of not being good enough and prepared enough, instead of preparation anxiety naturally required to be able to concentrate on the task. They could respond to this by overworking, judging themselves negatively and hiding their experience, thinking that it is a sign of lack of self-confidence. You could help them to reflect when it is more or less appropriate, showing the emotions and at the same time highlighting the importance of listening and valuing the internal experience as a natural response of our body in front of specific situations that can help to guide us through the process of what we have to do.

Guiding principles

Highlighting the importance of bodily experience.

Recognition of mismatch between behaviour and internal emotional experience.

Keeping in mind the difficulties in recognition of the internal emotional experience is important in understanding eating disorders.

Task 1.4:

I am going to ask you to think about the main character in your video. Can we talk about what you notice about the way they present themselves in the video?

The following prompts may help you to do this:

- Are they standing, sitting, do they move around, do they move quickly or slowly?
- Do they make eye contact with the camera, what are their facial expressions like?
- Do they use their hands or other parts of their body when they are talking?
- What are they saying, does the volume and tone of their voice change at all?

All of the above are aspects of non-verbal behaviours.

Notes for therapists to work with young people

Now try to think about any feelings they might be experiencing through the course of the video. What do you think s/he is feeling inside, also in regard to physical sensations?

Try to describe what you see and match it to emotions.

Can we talk about this together? Do you think the main character acts like this the whole time, do you think they have to make an effort to be like this, can you think of a time in your life where you presented as one way to the outside world but were feeling very different on the inside? Did you have to try to do this, did it take additional effort?

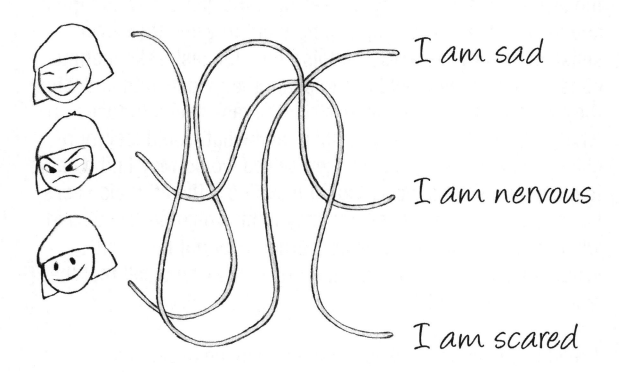

Behaviour can be misleading

Notes for therapists to work with young people

Task 1.5: Expressing your emotions into words
Notes for the therapist

Task four presents the idea of showing something different to the world than how we really feel inside. What we show on the outside can be incongruent with what we feel on the inside. Task five takes this a step further by asking the young person to engage with the idea of creating their own video and asks them to think about what they would like to communicate about themselves. This task is trying to support the young person to focus on their own subjective experience. The aim is to help the young person to focus on their own view and to sit with the anxiety this creates by not seeing it the same way as others and valuing the difference, helping them to value their own sense of agency. As a way of doing this, the task asks them to consider who they would like to share their video with and who they would like to value or "like" it. The task needs to focus on what they would find easy to share and what would feel more challenging, what aspects of themselves would they find it easy to share and what aspects would they find difficult. It also asks them to consider what aspects they think would be "liked" and what aspects they would be concerned may not be "liked". Would they feel able to share their own self or the self that they feel would be "liked"?

The idea behind the task is that there may be aspects of themselves that are very difficult to share, that they pretend aren't there or they keep hidden. When the young person is able to reflect on the influence of what they think are other people's expectations in how they present themselves, it would be important also to help them to consider what their

Notes for therapists to work with young people

own expectations are and the possible pressure they put on themselves to keep up with the idealised image they might have of themselves. For example, some young people expect never to make mistakes or be able to always be there for their peers. Reflecting on the impact of these self-beliefs in their emotions and actions will help them to better understand the function of the eating disorder symptoms.

Guiding principles

Keeping in mind that young people with eating disorders tend to over prioritise external values and what they think are others' expectations.

Being interested in understanding what is the idealised image that they have about themselves.

Encouraging the young person to be curious about their own experiences.

Encouraging the young person to tolerate their own experiences.

Encouraging them to reflect on what they feel comfortable sharing and what they prefer to keep private.

Task 1.5:

In this task, I would like you to think about making your own video. What do you feel would be important to share about yourself, what aspects of yourself would you like to share with the outside world? How would it feel to share these things?

Notes for therapists to work with young people

It may be easier to share some things and it may be harder to share others. What words would you struggle to share about yourself, would there be things that you might struggle to say?

Do you think your video would represent a whole picture of yourself or would some aspects remain off-camera?

Would you tell me more about the aspects that you would like to remain off-camera? Do you think that some aspects will remain off-camera because they do not match your own and other people's expectations?

Laura's story

Being in front of the judges

Laura is 15 years old; she was referred by her GP to Specialist CAMHS following weight loss and food restriction. She had

Notes for therapists to work with young people

some nutritional input from the dietician and gained some weight; however, she was really struggling with anorexic cognitions and was referred for individual therapy. Laura had not experienced any therapy prior to this. She worked through some of these tasks with her therapist for several weeks.

Laura was open to identifying a show that she has enjoyed watching. Interestingly, she identified a show that she was drawn to because it was short and did not get in the way of other tasks, so she could do things afterwards. Her initial reason for liking the show was because it was funny. The show was called *That's So Raven*, an American sitcom that she watched online.

It is about a girl who has psychic visions of what might happen in the future. In an attempt to try and make the visions come true or avoid them, she gets herself into trouble at home or school or with her friends. It's just funny.

Laura was able to describe her favourite episode when Raven had a vision that in the future, she would model her own dress design and would win a showcase in her favourite magazine only to find out that when she joined the show, they thought she was too big to model the dress and instead someone really skinny had been given the job. She was upset about it and tried her best to lose the weight within a week, which was not possible. Raven then made two dresses for a size six model and also one for herself. When it was showtime, against the rules, she comes out at the same time as the model. This displeased the judges and although disqualified, the photographers liked it. She was then escorted out by security.

Laura was able to share why she chose this episode:

Because it made it seem like it's okay to be a bit bigger. At the same time, the idea of it is quite scary and not always accepted. I know it's not realistic for me and I don't think I will ever get to be in that position.

Laura talked about liking the show because it was funny. She also talked about how it made her feel sad as well as it made her feel that when you are bigger people don't always like you. She also talked about not being able to fit into clothes in the same way when you are bigger. This touched on painful memories from when she saw herself as bigger before she lost weight.

Laura was also able to think about how this show would be without emotion. She talked about it not being as interesting or funny. She was able to connect with Raven's feelings because of the way she expressed herself both verbally and non-verbally, in terms of what she was saying and how she was saying it. Laura was able to see that without emotions in the show it wouldn't be as funny; she thought it may seem blank and the acting would seem terrible. She didn't think she would watch the show.

Laura identified herself with Raven in thinking about how the comments impacted on her self- confidence and self-esteem. She was able to identify with the idea of not showing her true feelings as that might not have seemed acceptable, and therefore hiding her true feelings to fit in with other peoples' expectations even though this made the character feel very sad. She also acknowledged that if the character had shown

Notes for therapists to work with young people

her true feelings the outcome may have been different and there was a feeling of loss and the need to pretend that everything was okay.

From the start of the task, Laura was able to talk about the task in relation to her body image. Some young people may be able to do this sooner than others, and in many ways, it is an indicator of readiness to work on specific issues. However, the process is as important as the content and if a young person chooses an example that is unrelated to their specific difficulties that can be valuable to explore too.

Through the process of the task, Laura was able to talk more about her achievements. These were the things she felt comfortable sharing; however, she struggled more to talk about her family situation, where her parents had recently separated. She was able to say that she was not ready to share this with anyone currently. She was also able to recognise that the family was in a fortunate position from a financial and social perspective, however, they still had their own difficulties and that people might not expect this. She began to engage with the idea that not everything that looks perfect from the outside is perfect on the inside.

Section 2 – The eating disorder filter

Overview

Section two focuses on helping the young person to recognise the challenges that their eating disorder brings. Here it would be important for the therapist to keep in mind specifically what is described in chapter two about the development of psychological distress in eating disorders and the "filter" analogy.

Notes for therapists to work with young people

The first task focuses on this in a practical/behavioural way by asking the young person to think about what they do differently because of their eating disorder. This may not be as easy as it sounds. For us as professionals it may be easy to recognise symptoms of an eating disorder. However, for young people, these behaviours have often become normal life and they don't always recognise that they are related to their disorder.

The first task is a gentle exercise discussing day-to-day life and opening up areas to potentially discuss where the eating disorder may be impacting. The task then moves onto asking the young person to imagine posting this video online and to think about what other people may think – so trying to introduce the idea of an alternative perspective, which can be a very helpful therapeutic tool. In task two the analogy is developed a little further with an emphasis on engaging the young person with their behaviour and to help them think about what they are happy for other people to see and what they would prefer to hide. At this stage, we are just focusing on eliciting behaviours that they would rather not share rather than thinking about the emotions behind them as that comes later. Task three focuses on the discrepancies between what they want people to see and what they are hiding, perhaps beginning to think about reasons for why they want to hide or not share certain aspects of their behaviour. The final two tasks in the section move the work on as the young person then begins to focus on the difficult behaviours or behaviours that they are not willing to share as the eating disorder part of their life. Task four begins to name eating disorder behaviours as symptoms and discusses further the impact of these symptoms, trying to elicit emotions related to this. Finally, task five uses the idea of a storyboard to support the young person to try and draw links between what it is they are feeling (emotion) and what they are doing (behaviour).

Notes for therapists to work with young people

Now that you have your timeline, can you tell me about the parts of the day you would like to film to make your video, or maybe you could tell me more about what will be in your video if we focused on yesterday? If you did post any part of your video online, who do you think would follow your video? Who would you want to follow your video? How would you describe the video at the moment? What would other people see (e.g. your parents, friends, teachers)?

How much of the daily routine that you have shared in your online video is influenced by your eating disorder? Do you think that people watching your video would notice this in any way?

Notes for therapists to work with young people

Task 2.2: Behind the scenes
Notes for the therapist

Task one focused on imaging to share a video diary online. This task goes one step further and asks the young person to imagine being behind the scenes at the making of their video. The aim of this task is to help the young person engage in the aspects of their daily life that they are not keen to share, the parts of their life that happen behind the scenes. If the young person is struggling to think about any discrepancies, the following may help as examples to help demonstrate this: the young person may show that they are confident in completing a school task in the video but they are unable to share that they spent hours puzzling over the details as that is the part that they do not want people to see, or they may share that they had lunch but they may not share that they took an hour to eat or skipped eating it. The task of the therapist is to try and elicit from the young person the things that they do not want people to see and to discuss the reasons why, enabling them to engage in the idea of a pretence or part of life that is hidden or they are too scared to show. It would be important to help them to understand that on one hand every one of us keeps certain aspects private. However, the difference here is that the eating disorder behaviours are maintained by unrealistic expectations and performances that have a detrimental effect on their psychological and physical wellbeing.

Guiding principles

Encouraging the young person to reflect on the image that they want to present to others and whether this image might be idealised and unrealistic.

Notes for therapists to work with young people

> Helping them to understand that the need behind this is related more to their need for social integration (e.g. feeling accepted, liked and helpful for others).
>
> Acknowledging the idea that the eating disorder can happen behind the scenes and the need for individuation (e.g. feeling unique and different from others; developing their own qualities and skills) becomes expressed through the eating disorder behaviour.

Task 2.2:

Now try to think about the video that you imagined making in task one. Imagine what you would like to review or edit from this video as if you were behind the scenes at the making of your video.

Do you think there are any discrepancies between what is happening and what other people may see when they watch the video?

What are the things that are happening that other people cannot see?

What are the things that are going wrong, or the things that you would want to edit? How do you feel about those things?

Do you think that anybody (e.g. parents, friends, teachers) are aware of this?

Notes for therapists to work with young people

Task 2.3: Keeping up the performance
Notes for the therapist

This task aims to discuss in more detail the discrepancies talked about in the last task, but also to focus on the impact of these on the overall performance, how the young person might come across in the video and the style of the video. The aim of the task is to help the young person identify that there are discrepancies and that they do impact what is really happening. For example, the perfectionist approach towards school work is now making them feel obsessive and exhausted, or continually not eating lunch is making them feel miserable. The continuous hiding of the truth is making them feel guilty about pretending. It may be helpful for the therapist to help them explore in more detail the costs of

Notes for therapists to work with young people

keeping up the performance or the emotional and physical effort of continually hiding how things really are. This task presents the opportunity to further explore and improve awareness of the idealised image of self, influenced by their own expectations about themselves and also what they think are external expectations. It is important for the therapist to continue to keep in mind how this idealised image acts as a filter preventing young people to further develop their self.

Guiding principles

Introduction of the idea of the balance of two separate needs – social integration and individualisation.

Focusing on the over-investment in the need for perfected social performance based on an idealised image of themselves.

Helping them to notice that being over-invested in the "performance" will cause distress (e.g. obsessiveness and rumination).

Task 2.3:

I would like you to take a few minutes to think about the discrepancies that we have been talking about in the last task, so the things that happen that you don't want to show.

Holding in mind your video, do you think that the discrepancies that you notice in the making of the video ever impact the overall story or performance? If you were now able to think about this video in relation to your wider life, do you think there is a cost of keeping up the story or the performance?

Notes for therapists to work with young people

Can you think of a time when the cost has been too great, or a time when managing your behaviours has been difficult?

Can you think about how you felt at that moment?

Did you feel that you had to reorganise things?

Try to identify how you have managed feelings. When you watch your playlist, what behaviour can you identify that helped you to manage feelings? Were they helpful or unhelpful behaviours?

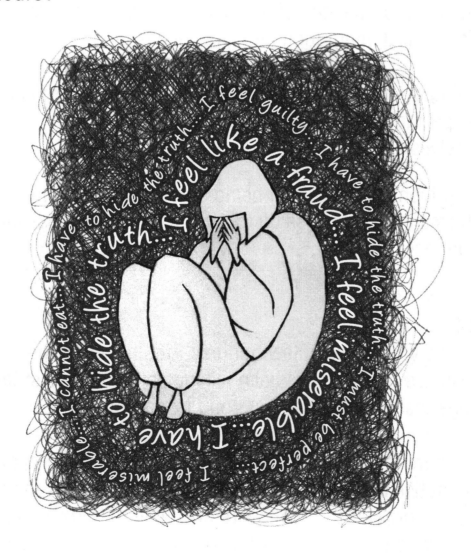

Notes for therapists to work with young people

Task 2.4: The eating disorder magnifying glass
Notes for the therapist

The final two tasks of this section move on considerably – they are the first two tasks in the workbook that have *eating disorder* in the title.

The purpose of task four is to help the young person explore the impact that their eating disorder symptoms have on their routine and the way they choose to do things on a daily basis, so beginning to explore the cycle of their illness. The first step of the therapist is to help the young person recognise their behaviours as symptoms. The eating disorder behaviours may have become very enmeshed in normal life for the young person, so separating this out is an important aspect of the task. Once the behaviours have been separated out as symptoms, the discussion can then move onto thinking about how the behaviours/symptoms are impacting. The final part of the task is to help the young person link the behaviour/symptom to emotions, to help them reflect on what emotions are triggering the behaviour and also what emotion is created by the behaviour.

Guiding principles

Helping young people to recognise their eating disorder behaviours as unhelpful, therefore as symptoms.

Recognition of the impact that eating disorder symptoms have in their day-to-day life.

Notes for therapists to work with young people

> Encouraging links between eating disorder behaviours and emotions, being mindful that the eating disorder can act as a coping mechanism to regulate emotions.

Task 2.4:

Can you think about what aspects of your behaviour are influenced by your eating disorder symptoms and how does this impact your decisions about what to show in your video? What do the eating disorder symptoms lead you to do exactly?

If you focused on a specific day of your week, would you be able to do a very up-close shot and zoom in on your behaviours? What can you see? Thinking about this specific day, would you be able to try drawing your own sequence or storyboard of behaviour, trying to make links between emotion and behaviour?

Did your ways of managing help you to understand the emotion you were feeling in that moment on that day or was it a way of avoiding the emotion – what was easier in that moment?

How effective were these ways of managing for you and the people around you?

What emotions did your unhelpful behaviours create? How intensely did you experience these emotions? They may have been stronger or more unpredictable, at times they may have been overwhelming.

148

Notes for therapists to work with young people

Task 2.5: Removing the eating disorder filter – a language for behaviour

Notes for the therapist

This task builds on the storyboard idea more. The aim is to help the young person understand the link between behaviour and emotion and how they use their behaviour to hide their emotion; showing the real emotion can feel too revealing, contradict the narrative that they think people hold about them or indeed their own narrative about what is acceptable. Working through the storyboard, ask the young person to try and link their eating disorder behaviours to emotion. Then ask the young person to think about what might happen if they didn't engage in that particular behaviour. Which emotions would they show and what would they do instead to manage the emotion? For example, if they identified restricting food as the behaviour, the young person might want to think about when this happens, such as

Notes for therapists to work with young people

when they are angry with parents or when they are anxious about school performance. Then the therapist can explore the idea of not engaging in that behaviour. For example, if they didn't engage in the food restriction what would they express differently and what aspects of their behaviour would they find difficult, socially unacceptable or just too challenging to show to the outside world?

Guiding principles

The ideas of "Identity Zero" and "the eating disorder as a filter" are relevant here.

Both concepts can help the young person to engage in the idea of life without their eating disorder. At the same time recognising the value of the eating disorder to suppress the negative emotion.

Task 2.5:

Thinking again about the sequence of behaviour or storyboard that you have created, can you think about the emotions that may be associated with each sequence of the story? If you couldn't use any of these behaviours, and you only had language to express yourself, what would you have said to the people around you, your friends and family? Let's try to write this down as a message together.

What emotions are you able to express freely?

Do you think the eating disorder gets in the way of how you express your feelings?

Are there other things that get in the way too?

Notes for therapists to work with young people

Would you be able to name any of the emotions that you feel you cannot show? Why do you think some emotions are hidden? Do you think you would be worried about other people's judgements if you didn't hide some of these emotions?

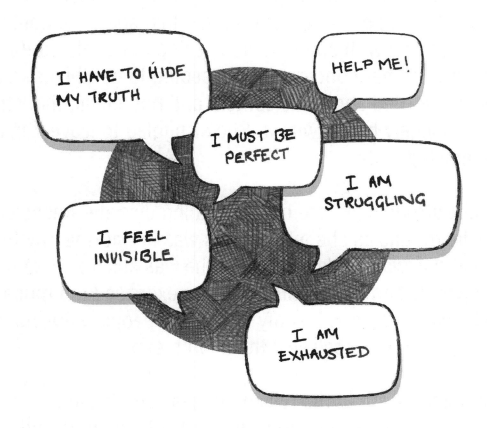

Laura's story

The emotions hidden behind a "perfect life"

Laura was able to describe her daily routine and she acknowledged that part of her behaviour pattern involved restricting food. However, this was described in a very factual way and there was no emotional expression related to these behaviours at this stage in the work. She was also able to openly list other behaviours that might have been related to her eating disorder such as exercising several times a day.

Laura was able to engage in conversation about who she felt she would want to watch her video. She shared apprehension about her father watching the video as she felt that he didn't really engage in this type of activity or conversation. She also acknowledged that she would only be comfortable with some friends seeing it, not all. Laura demonstrated her concern about needing to get things right by being worried about the content and not feeling that she was completely happy with it. She struggled to leave it in an uncompleted state.

She also struggled to see how the eating disorder impacted her daily routine as she felt that this was her normal rhythm and that this was working for her. She was able to share that some people had commented that she exercised too much but she was unable to identify who these people were and the extent to which she believed their comments.

When thinking about the review process and talking about the discrepancies between what is happening and what people are seeing when they watch the video, Laura struggled to acknowledge aspects of her behaviour that troubled people.

Some people have said I exercise too much. To me, three hours is not that much and it's just so that I keep fit. Also, some people might think that I need to eat more. My friends have said how my lunch is too little and they don't understand why I only have a salad. It's what I like to eat and it keeps my body healthy. They may think I am a loner too because I am mostly by myself but I do like my own space.

Notes for therapists to work with young people

Laura talked about the pressure of being seen in a certain way in relation to her family situation.

My family situation. It's a lot and I try my best to cover it. I am sure everyone thinks it's all okay if you asked. They would describe us as the perfect people with everything that we need.

They may not see what I see. I see myself as quite big, especially my stomach and legs. Everyone says about how skinny I am.

When talking about making changes or edits to the video Laura struggled to think about how to make these changes without feeling a degree of discomfort, she was not yet able to discuss this in terms of her eating disorder.

I don't want to change my routine though because this will make me feel uncomfortable and quite stressed.

Laura was able to engage in a discussion relating to the pressure of keeping up the performance. She talked about feeling exhausted by the effort to pretend that everything is fine when really on the inside things were far from fine. Laura, through the process of talking about discrepancies, was able to acknowledge the pain and anguish that this created particularly in relation to trying to hide the difficulties in her parent's relationship. She was able to talk about how this made her feel emotionally.

I just wanted to get through the day and to do everything I was expected to do so no one would guess something was wrong. Honestly, I wanted to fast forward but couldn't.

Through the process of talking about the pain, she also talked about how hard she tried to suppress her feelings and how not eating had become a way to help her feel better.

By focusing on a specific day, Laura was able to start making the link between emotion and behaviour.

Table 4.1 *Example of Laura's chart*

	Activity/ Ongoing	Emotion	Behaviour	Emotion
6:00 – 8:00	Woke up Exercised (50 sit ups, 30 squats) Shower and got ready	In control of what I was doing	Exercise	Happy
8:00 – 8:30	Breakfast	Calm	Eat cereal bar	Okay
8:30 – 9:00	Dad comes to take me to school and is late. Mom and dad argue.	Frustrated inside	Left them and went to the car	Sad Angry Lonely
9:00 – 11:00	15 mins late for school. Dad complaining about mum in the car.	Angry Upset Tired Anxious	Kept quiet and listened	Angry Upset Tired Anxious

Notes for therapists to work with young people

	Activity/ Ongoing	Emotion	Behaviour	Emotion
11:30 – 13:00	Lesson: French, English Mathematics	Worried about upcoming exam	Revised Maths	Worried Unprepared Frustrated Sad
13:00 – 14:00	Lunch - didn't eat my salad	Worried Sad	Revised Maths Left my friends in canteen	Worried that time is running out
17:00 – 18:00	Gym	Feel like it's going well	Exercised	Feel fit and happier
18:00 – 19:00	Gymnastics	Happy at the beginning	Fell off the beam	Sad Upset Failure Disappoint-ment
19:30 – 20:00	Dinner	Upset	Ate half my meal	Upset
20:00 – 22:00	Slept early 21:00	Tired Upset Failure		

Laura talked about not wanting to deal with the emotion but just wanting to keep busy and occupied. She talked about not eating as a way of feeling better and more in control of her feelings. She was able to start distinguishing between feelings and made the following list relating to hidden emotions.

> *Hidden emotions:*
>
> *Angry: Everyone expects me to be the calm person. And I don't want to be seen like an angry person.*
>
> *Sad: I can show this at home a bit. Not outside though as people then will know there are things going on.*
>
> *Anxious: I don't want to be asked why I am worried.*
>
> *Happiness: I don't show this as much because things are not always okay. I prefer to remain neutral.*

Section 3 – Making your playlist

Overview

Now that the young person and therapist have established what behaviours contribute to the eating difficulties and have started to explore the links between these behaviours and the emotions behind them, it is time to move the young person onto considering the historical development of their difficulties. An important part of the therapy journey is to be able to look back and identify moments in time when the behaviours that make up the eating disorder started. Initially, the process may focus on practical time indicators such as a certain year, a certain month, a time of transition from one school year to another school year or a period of loss. The young person may not necessarily link the time frame with the development of the eating difficulties as they may just identify this time as a difficult time or a time when they seemed to feel worried or upset. It is important that the therapist does not infer that particular situation or event that caused the eating disorder.

Notes for therapists to work with young people

It is unlikely to be as clear and concise as that in the young person's mind; moreover, we know that the causes of eating disorders are multifactorial. However, it is important to help the young person to think about the meaning of the situation/stage/transition in terms of the development of their own identity. For example, there may have been a time when the young person wanted to express and develop themselves more, however, they felt too anxious for fear of not matching other people's expectations of them, or what they perceived those expectations to be.

The first task is a very practical application of this process. Using the analogy of a playlist of videos, the young person is asked to think about ordering events in the same way as they may order a playlist, the ordering process being the framework to aid the linking of events, emotions and behaviours. Task two builds on this by then asking the young person to think about "unexpected scenes" as a way of discussing events/situations that may have been difficult or that weren't necessarily planned for. The concept of "unexpected" is important here as it is often the unexpected aspects of life that we human beings struggle to manage most; times when we didn't anticipate the emotion we experienced, times when our feelings surprised us or distressed us or times when we felt out of control. Often, it is not the event itself that is challenging but the way we interpret it and, therefore, the emotions that we feel. It is important that the young person is able to enter into a dialogue about this, as it is the "unexpectedness" of emotion that has caused the fracture or displacement and to recognise that it is not just difficult because it is unexpected but because the situation might have led to the emergence of new needs and values. The young person needs to recognise that by resisting the change they did not know how to then incorporate those new needs and values into their life.

The final three tasks in this section build further on the analogy by using the idea of exploring "highlights" referring to what went well (task three). For highlights, we refer to situations, memories and relationships where the young people felt welcomed, accepted and understood in their emotional experience and view. As suggested in chapter two, we would suggest shifting from the vulnerability/diathesis-stress model towards the environmental sensitivity meta-framework, which takes into account the interaction between both negative and positive environments and the specific characteristics and temperament of the person. It is important to consider that each young person can respond differently to situational and relational scenarios based on where they are in the sensitivity trait continuum, so on their temperament. This will impact what they have had experienced as "unexpected" and "highlights" scenes.

Discussing the concept of different versions for different people (task four) is an important aspect as it links back to the earlier idea of Identity Three where the two basic needs are more in balance, and Identity Zero, stuck within the filter.

Finally, task five brings the section to a close with a review and check-in exercise to ensure that the young person is on board with the concepts and engaged in the process. Again, the idea of the analogy is used to think about connectiveness and how connected the young person may feel to the playlist as it stands. This ultimately represents how connected they feel to the story and how engaged they are in the therapy.

Notes for therapists to work with young people

Task 3.1: Making your playlist
Notes for the therapist

This task is the first task in this section. It focuses on how the eating disorder developed, so the order of the story. The analogy of a "playlist of videos" is used to help the young person engage in the idea of ordering the development of events. The therapist's task is to help the young person think about what events feel significant and how these events developed over a period of time. Here, the development of events is not seen in a cause-effect sense, rather we would like to emphasise the importance of telling their story within a safe therapeutic relationship, where together with the therapist the young people can attribute new meanings to what they have experienced.

Also, for each separate video, it would be helpful to identify a main theme and the emotions connected with it. It might be helpful to ask the young person to choose a title that would reflect the theme for each video. Identifying themes and choosing a title could help them find out more about what they value in their story and the interconnection between them.

Guiding principles

This task moves to the "here and now", transitioning from the third person to a personal perspective.

The idea focuses on storytelling and the story of how the eating disorder might have developed.

The narrative is represented by the "Making a playlist", enabling the young person to link emotions and events.

159

Notes for therapists to work with young people

Task 3.1:
In this task, I would like you to think about the idea of a "playlist of videos", which relates to different events that may have happened in your life that feel significant to you. These can be events taken from any stage of your life, it doesn't have to be just recent history. We can try to order these events together. How did you feel at that time? Can you identify emotions that might be linked to those events?

What title would you give to your playlist of videos?

Do you have a clear idea of how the playlist would go?

Notes for therapists to work with young people

Task 3.2: Unexpected scenes
Notes for the therapist

This task builds on from task one by asking the young person to start to make links between significant events and the development of their eating disorder. The analogy is used to help convey this idea as the concept of "unexpected scenes" in their video playlist. In the overview we described what we mean by "unexpected scenes" and it is important to explain this concept to the young person; exploring the idea that there might be events in their playlist that were unexpected and challenging. It is the challenges that these events created internally for the young person that will have led to things going unexpectedly off track. Exploring this in more detail aims to help link what was happening in their lives to the development of eating disorder symptoms as a way of managing the unexpected emotions they experienced at that time. For example, once a young person who was 19 years old recalled that when she was about 11 years old her mother told her that she could become a very good medical doctor like her when older. The mother did not mean that that was what she expected from her daughter, but it was her way to highlight her empathic understanding and analytical skills. The young person interpreted that phrase as an encouragement to be like her mother and focused on that instead of exploring what she liked. When she said this in therapy, she was at the beginning of her first year in medicine. She had started suffering from bulimia nervosa in her last high school year. This memory with the analysis of other dynamics helped us to understand more the function of the eating disorder and to put this into the context of her story.

Notes for therapists to work with young people

Guiding principles

Focus on challenging or unexpected events, times of transitions and memories.

Presentation of the emerging conflict between social integration and individuation needs.

This is not the idea of a specific trigger or trauma but rather a continuous lived experience that was uncomfortable.

Task 3.2:

Let's think back to the video playlist that you created in task one. Are there any videos where you can begin to see things becoming more challenging? Or maybe memories of specific situations that were particularly meaningful for you and created a sort of pressure?

At what point in the playlist do you notice them? Were you aware this was happening at the time or can you see it more when you look back? What events do you think contributed to this? Who noticed that it was going off track?

Are there some events that you feel may be linked to the development of your eating disorder? Do these events have any common themes or common people?

Notes for therapists to work with young people

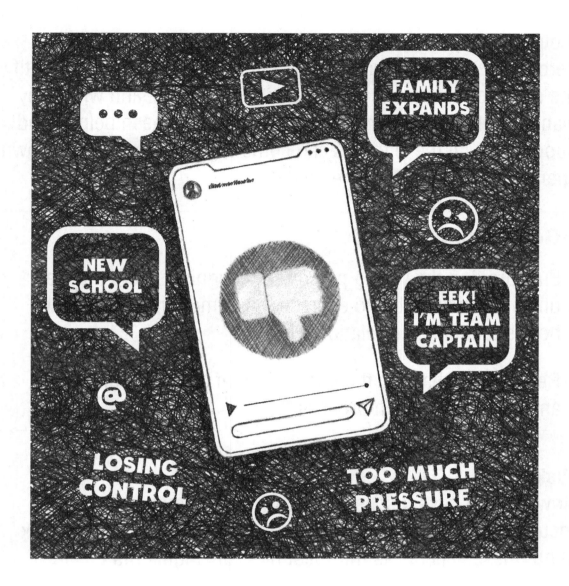

Task 3.3: Watching the highlights

Notes for the therapist

This task aims to encourage the young person to focus on positive events and meaningful relationships as "highlights". As mentioned in the overview, highlights are referred to as situations, memories and relationships where the young people felt welcomed, accepted and understood in their emotional experience and view. Recalling and focusing on these moments can help them to feel more connected to other people and more supported. It is also a way to help them to counterbalance

Notes for therapists to work with young people

their tendency towards self-criticism and the experience or perception of feeling judged. It is important to help them identify the common themes in the things that went well and what they want to hold onto in terms of things that have been helpful and supportive. All these things can come together to form their own "personal highlights" of their video.

> **Guiding principles**
>
> Encouraging the young person to recognise where they felt understood and able to express their emotions, focusing on both situations and relationships.
>
> Relating this back to the importance of a balance of needs and the individuation process.

Task 3.3:

Now that we have discussed what went off track, we want to focus on what went well. Therefore, we would like you to think about these aspects as the "best bits" or "highlights".

What were some of the highlights before and after the eating disorder, which stood out for you?

If you asked your parents or friends to describe some highlights too, do you think they would describe the same things?

Are you able to hold different views from the people around you? Which highlights would you choose to hold onto and save to watch again?

164

Notes for therapists to work with young people

Task 3.4: Different versions of your playlist

Notes for the therapist

The aim of this task is for the young person to try and identify the discrepancies between how they told their story and what things other people noticed in their story. To continue with the use of the analogy in the task, we talk about different versions of the playlist. In this task, we can ask the young person to explore different points of view such as those of friends or family members. Try to encourage

Notes for therapists to work with young people

the young person to think about the expectations of others around them and how these may have been different from their own expectations. Here it might be helpful to revisit Robert's story as described in chapter three. This was a central passage in his therapy as he had to review his father's story, career as a doctor and potential expectations on him as well as understanding his own values in regard to the doctor that he wanted to become.

> **Guiding principles**
>
> Emphasis on the importance of highlighting different views and valuing them as opposed to adapting to whatever is valued as the presentable norm.
>
> Focus on the tendency to adapt, relating to the need to prioritise other people and their needs/expectations over their own.
>
> Drawing on the overemphasis on external validation in the presentation of eating disorders.

Task 3.4:

Having explored both the things that went off track and the things that you chose as highlights in your playlist, try now to think about how other people might view your playlist. Would they make the same choices as you or would theirs be different? If they made different choices how would you rationalise these in your own mind?

Notes for therapists to work with young people

Task 3.5: Connecting to your playlist
Notes for the therapist

The final task of this section aims to bring together all the other tasks and review the process. This task is an opportunity to "check in" and see how it feels to do this. Try to encourage the young person to think about taking ownership of their story and how they might direct change with their own response and the people around them. The idea of this is to help the young person acknowledge their authentic feelings about situations rather than just going along with other people's views.

> **Guiding principles**
>
> Consolidation of ideas and prioritising their values.
>
> Identity Zero and the eating disorder filter being part of a development process that was hard.
>
> Valuing your own experience of this process.

Task 3.5:
This task brings us to the end of section three. It would be nice to "pause" and "check in" with how it feels to talk about your experiences in this way.

Think about your own playlist, what feelings does this provoke for you? Do you consider them as positive or negative?

Now that you have been able to identify when things started to go off track and also the things that you wanted to save as highlights, imagine that you have the opportunity to review your playlist with a hopeful outcome. In the rewritten version, what felt important for you at that time? What were the main themes you wanted other people to notice? What would need to change? Would you involve different people or would you direct people differently? Would you be able to separate your views from the people around you and do things differently?

Notes for therapists to work with young people

Laura's story

Exploring the emotions behind her playlist

Laura was very creative when it came to thinking about the idea of a playlist. She chose the title name "The Other Side", which was very thoughtful. Laura was able to think about different scenes in her playlist of videos that were important to her. These events were significant experiences in her life.

Scene 1: My lost baby brother
Scene 2: My father's cheating
Scene 3: My parents separating
Scene 4: Moving in with my mother

By using the analogy of the playlist, Laura was able to move back and forth through the different scenes and was able to think about more challenging times. Laura was able to talk about the events and link the feelings together giving her some sense of order, whereas before it felt very chaotic. From this point, Laura was then able to think about when her behaviour around eating changed. She pinpointed her Dad leaving the family home as a time when she started to eat less. She felt guilty for the anger and disappointment she had towards her Dad. She started to go to the gym as a way of keeping busy and then joined a gymnastics club, not really being able to focus on her emotional experience at that time. She became very focused on being good at things rather than having to deal with other difficult emotions. These behaviours were a way to compensate for and clear the difficult feelings she had about her family situation. For a while, she was only able to have a black-and-white approach, finding it difficult

---

169

to hold the nuances of positive and negative feelings we can have towards people close to us.

Alongside thinking about things that got very difficult, Laura was also able to think about what went well. Laura talked about personal memories of happy occasions, fun things that involved all the family. She was also able to think about before and after events and before and after feelings, and therefore, really beginning to make links between some of her emotional experiences and her responses to things. Laura was able to hold in mind other people's perspectives and so was able to acknowledge that people around her may have seen things differently to her. Laura acknowledged that sometimes this was easier than others and it was also dependent on who it was, showing some insight into the impact relationships can have on the way we respond to things as well.

Laura acknowledged that being able to think about events and link emotions to it was a way of being able to understand her feelings more. She talked about it all feeling like a bit of a blur and then some order being imposed through the process of trying to list events and responses. Laura was able to take on board that other people may have seen things differently and that she may have felt under pressure to respond a certain way so that she appeared okay, or so that it seemed like she was coping with some of the challenges that the family was facing. It also helped her to see that even though there were really challenging times, there were nice times and happy memories too. This enabled her to have a more integrated and complex view of some events and also of the people around her.

Notes for therapists to work with young people

Section 4 – New playlist, new self

Overview

This section of the workbook heralds "new beginnings" and the aim is to support the young person to engage more fully with their Identity Three, as described in chapter two, rather than focus on trying to keep up the habits needed to be in the Identity Zero. This refers back to the concept of "individuation" that was discussed in chapter two. All of the tasks in this section promote openness and honesty, and encourage authenticity with emotions, something that in the past may have felt too difficult. To be able to engage in the tasks presented in section four, there needs to be a degree of acceptance that change is very much needed and wanted. The therapeutic space needs to be safe and containing to enable the bravery and courage required in terms of trying to engage in doing something new, something that is different from what has been done in the past.

The first task in this section is about engaging the young person to think about a new playlist of videos, something that represents how they might be feeling now in the present. To support containment, the young person does not necessarily need to share this task with the therapist but is asked to reflect on the process of doing it. We are asking the young person to engage in the process of doing and thinking about something new.

Task two builds on this further by asking the young person to think about the content of their playlist, examining their reasons for choosing this. This task is quite challenging and there are prompts to support the young person in their thinking in relation to this.

171

Notes for therapists to work with young people

The final three tasks are focused on alternative perspectives. They introduce the idea of other people's views on the playlist, what it might be like to share something like this and who would it feel safe to share with. These encourage the young person to allow other people to engage in their "new self/ Identity Three".

Task five brings the section to a close with a task that's focused on rediscovery; what has the young person rediscovered about themselves? It may be a quality they forgot they had or something that they have learnt about themselves through this experience. Ideally, this section will end on a positive discussion of qualities that the young person had not thought about in some time or perhaps never, so ending on the idea that new challenges bring new opportunities and new ways of being that can enable positive and long-lasting change.

Some parts of these tasks can be done during the session, encouraging the young person to reflect on themes and patterns that could be represented in the playlist of videos. The young person could be invited to continue working on the videos on their own and then discuss their experience in the following session with their therapist.

Task 4.1: Rebranding your playlist
Notes for the therapist

This task aims to help the young person engage in the idea of a new playlist of videos that represents how they are feeling in the present. This playlist can be private and they don't need to share the contents with the therapist; however, it would be helpful if they were able to share themes and patterns that they may have noticed.

Notes for therapists to work with young people

It would also be helpful to try and encourage them to think about the experience of doing this task; how did it feel to be open and honest, was it a new experience, did it leave them feeling vulnerable and exposed, was it empowering? They must understand that they don't need to share the content of their playlist with you as the therapist, because the key part of the task is to help them engage with being open and honest with themselves.

Guiding principles

Encouraging openness and authenticity with emotions, asking the young person to think about a new playlist of videos without the eating disorder filter.

Encouraging the transition from Identity Zero to Identity Three – prioritisation of individual needs.

Encouraging a safe, open space to do this.

Task 4.1:

Think about making the first intro video in your playlist. You will be the only one to watch this. How does it feel to be able to be completely open about yourself? What would you say about how you are feeling in the here and now?

How easy was it to be open and honest about how you were feeling?

I would like you to make your video at home, or if you don't like the idea of making the video you can write the script. When we meet again we can talk about your experience of doing this task.

Did it make you feel vulnerable and exposed, or was it empowering for you? How do you think you could begin to build this style of thinking into your life on a more regular basis?

Task 4.2: New content in your playlist
Notes for the therapist

Building on task one, this task aims to help the young person think more about the content of their playlist of videos. In the previous task, themes and patterns were talked about but this task focuses more on the details, helping the young person to

Notes for therapists to work with young people

analyse the themes and to try to understand more about the patterns and why they are there. These themes and patterns can be thought about on several different levels; main topics and values, qualities that the young person may attribute to the themes and possible discrepancies between their personal views and other people's views. It is important to allow the young person to share any judgements that they feel will be made in relation to this content. Often, young people are very concerned that they will be judged in relation to any changes they may make to their behaviour or attitudes or any way in which they may deviate from an expectation.

Guiding principles

Drawing on the idea of individuation and encouraging young people to think about their values.

Presenting the idea of possible discrepancies and the need to build a tolerance to them.

Introducing the idea of acceptance and managing people's expectations rather than adapting to them.

Task 4.2:
Did you allow yourself the freedom to engage completely in this task?

What were the main themes or scenes that you wanted to show?

Were there negative and positive expressions? Did you focus on yourself or were you more concerned about other people's judgements or expectations? Were there barriers to how well you could allow yourself to do this? Are you able to think about what those barriers may have been?

Task 4.3: How would other people hear your playlist?

Notes for the therapist

This task moves the thinking on from private thinking that doesn't need to be shared to thinking about how other people may react to the young person's new playlist and how these views may impact. Who would be the key people for that young person and why would their view be so important? The aim of the task is to help the young person engage with the idea of being open and honest whilst feeling safe enough to do this. Would there be limits on how honest they could be? Are there people in their life who they wouldn't be able to be open and honest with, and what gets in the way of that? This could relate to not meeting expectations or it could relate to disappointing people.

Notes for therapists to work with young people

> **Guiding principles**
>
> Sharing all the vulnerabilities you might expose when you present yourself more openly.
>
> Developing an awareness of how much we want to expose depending on situational and relationship factors.
>
> Introducing the idea of a "limit" in terms of the personal cost to our own identity.

Task 4.3:

How do you think other people in your life would react to your new playlist?

Do you think you would have new followers?

How would you feel about other people seeing these videos?

Would you want some privacy settings in place or would you feel able to be open with it?

Would you block someone from seeing it completely?

Notes for therapists to work with young people

Task 4.4: Sharing your playlist

Notes for the therapist

This task is about trying to encourage the young person to share this playlist with someone important in their life. It is about trying to prepare them to share and manage their own fear of the response in a positive way. The young person may not be able to engage in this task at this stage and it is important to be able to think with the young person about their ambivalence and what this represents. These are the barriers to the young person accepting and sharing their own view of themselves and being able to engage in moving forward.

Guiding principles

Introducing the idea of sharing and reviewing with important people in our lives.

Supporting the idea of self-reflection and self-awareness in terms of getting needs met within relationships.

Task 4.4:

Think about the important people in your life. How easy would it be to share this playlist with them? Is this something you could do?

It is not always easy to be open and your real views may be difficult and may challenge the key people in your life. How would you manage this?

Notes for therapists to work with young people

Who are the people you think would be able to understand and welcome your openness? What might get in the way of you being able to communicate your real views?

Task 4.5: Presenting your own self

Notes for the therapist

The aim of this task is to help the young person to retain some of the qualities that they have rediscovered about themselves, to encourage them to keep being open and honest with themselves and if possible, with people around them. It is important to help them reflect on the emotions that might lead them to engage in unhelpful behaviours again and how they can engage with these emotions, but not with the unhelpful behaviours.

Notes for therapists to work with young people

> **Guiding principles**
>
> Consolidating the idea of being loyal to your own values.
>
> Demonstrating to others that you can hold your own ideas and identity with great value.
>
> Recognising difficult situations where the capacity to be loyal to yourself may be challenged due to social pressures.

Task 4.5:

What would you need to keep doing, to be able to present your own self?

Do you think you would ever slip back to the safety of the eating disorder filter?

What would be the warning signs or the red flags that might suggest you are struggling? How would you ensure you are able to maintain your own self-position?

What would need to happen within your family and friends to enable you to be able to maintain this position?

Notes for therapists to work with young people

Laura's story

The difficult process of starting a conversation with others

Laura found the idea of thinking about a playlist helpful as it enabled her to link her emotions to things that had happened. That being said, it was still very difficult for Laura to be truly open with herself as this was something that she hadn't done before and she felt vulnerable and exposed. She didn't open up completely to herself either; it was a gentle, step-by-step process that she engaged in gradually.

Laura talked about feeling vulnerable and exposed through the process of the therapy, as this was something she had never done before. This is a very hard stage of therapy to work through and it is at this point that many people give up and leave the therapy, feeling like it wasn't helpful. However, the strength of the therapeutic alliance is key in keeping the young person engaged even though it feels difficult. If there is enough trust within the relationship a young person can begin to work through their doubts and fears.

Prior to this, there had been no need to work through these difficult things as the eating difficulties had always been a source of protection that kept the difficult feelings in check. Now that this was identified as a problem, it felt like she had lost the thing that made her feel safe. Laura was desperate to have more understanding and other ways of coping now that she was able to acknowledge and understand that the eating disorder hadn't been solving any problems, but rather adding to more problems in the long term.

I felt vulnerable and exposed and I wanted to give up and go home and never come back to therapy as it was just getting too difficult. But I also felt listened to and that hadn't happened in a long time. This felt new and positive and it was that feeling that kept me coming back to the sessions.

Although at first it felt strange for Laura to be open, she tried to share as much as possible about what was going on. She identified her parents' separation as the longest scene in her playlist and how Dad moving out of the family home had a real impact. She reordered her playlist of videos to reflect how she felt about things and how it related to her experience more.

Video 1: How we were like before
Video 2: Losing the baby brother
Video 3: My parents' separation
Video 4: My eating disorder
Video 5: Letting go of the pain and the eating disorder
Video 6: My plans for the future
Video 7: The memories I will always treasure

In this way, Laura was more able to focus on herself, what she saw and how she felt. There were some barriers, for example, she didn't want her parents to feel guilty and she didn't want them to argue. She was tempted to revert back and minimise her feelings for their sake. She was worried about how they might see things and how this might feel for them.

She recognised that the eating disorder was a way to protect herself from opening a dialogue with other people, like her

Notes for therapists to work with young people

parents, due to her fear of sharing difficult feelings. The work conducted through these tasks was an opportunity to reflect on the importance of finding a mediation between her feelings and views and those of other people. However, whilst Laura was scared about how people would react, she decided she did want to share this with her parents, maybe specific scenes in the videos. This was a brave and promising start.

My parents can watch it but I won't want to be there until Videos 5 to 7. It won't be easy for me to share the first couple of videos as it will really show them what I think and how I felt.

Laura talked about changing her mind about what to share with who. It was a big decision and quite hard to think about, as she was so used to not sharing and managing her own feelings by herself. As part of the work, the temptation to slip back was talked about openly. Laura was finding the process hard and the temptation to step back into doing what she has always done was very strong. Together Laura and the therapist discussed the idea of slipping back and what this would mean for the eating disorder and how sometimes it can be part of the process of recovery.

Section 5 – Breaking free from the eating disorder filter

Overview

Section five is the last section in the workbook and focuses on consolidating the work and moving forward with what has been learnt. The integration of individual needs with the social world

Notes for therapists to work with young people

and the fine balance that is needed to ensure psychological wellbeing was discussed in chapter two, and this section attempts to help the young person to focus on this integration. The idea is to support young people to establish new healthy boundaries and recognise their sensitivity as a resource that has to be valued and respected. The tasks focus on supporting the young person to think about new skills they may have an awareness of, that may help them to keep moving forward and maintain and consolidate their new position of being in a changed place. The focus is on breaking free from the eating disorder and moving on in the hope that what is being moved onto is far more positive and encouraging.

The first task involves thinking about what they might notice if they were slipping back and how this could be shared openly with important people in their life so they can be involved in this too. It's about recognising slips and trying to address them positively and limit their impact. Task two is about reconnecting with peers and what impact this can have. Through the course of being unwell peer relationships can become disconnected, and it is important to recognise the difficulties this can cause. It may be that aspects of the reconnecting can be difficult and tricky and connecting with peers can, for some, trigger old habits and behaviour. Therefore, it is important that the young person is encouraged to reconnect with their Identity Three rather than slipping back to presenting their Identity Zero with the eating disorder filter.

Task three builds on this, asking the young person to think about the importance of a "comfort zone", encouraging them to think about what they are comfortable with and when they feel a level of discomfort and giving them strategies to be able to manage

Notes for therapists to work with young people

this. At the same time, this task acknowledges the importance of knowing their feelings rather than having to carry on regardless, which may have been a past strategy.

Tasks four and five focus on ending. Task four is about future aspirations. The future does not necessarily have to be defined in the task, it could be tomorrow, next week or next year. It is more about moving away from the past to something new and sharing some thoughts about that. Finally, we come to the final task in the book. We felt it was very important to support the idea of not having to share everything all of the time. Task five focuses on this by promoting the idea of private space and the value and importance of it. The workbook has encouraged sharing and reflection, but we also want to promote the idea that within our own thinking processes we can have a private space that is just for us; not everything needs to be shared and that has a great value too.

Task 5.1: Emotional talk with your family
Notes for the therapist

This section focuses on helping the young person to consolidate the changes they have talked about in earlier sections and think about what might put these changes at risk and how to avoid slipping back into established patterns of unhelpful behaviours. In terms of the analogy that has been featured in earlier sections, this section now focuses on not seeing things through the eating disorder filter. The aim is to encourage the young person to think about themselves without the eating disorder, so investing less in the eating disorder filter and focusing more on how they present themselves in the real-life world.

Notes for therapists to work with young people

Guiding principles

Promoting the idea of emotional sharing.

Emphasising the importance of reintegration of social and individuation needs.

Thinking about this more broadly and how it can be applied to other systems or situations in your life.

Together with your therapist create a Tip Sheet/Helpful Hints list for your family and friends with information about what you think they need to be aware of to help you maintain the changes you have made.

On the Tip Sheet/Helpful Hints include a section that applies to "Things to be avoided/unhelpful things". The Tip Sheet can focus on broader aspects of behaviour too, such as on your approach or the approach that people take towards you and what you find helpful/unhelpful about that.

For example: You don't find it helpful to have Mum following you around to check that you are managing but you do like to share time with Mum in a supportive way.

Once you have completed your list, think about how you could share this with important family and friends so you can work towards a shared understanding.

Notes for therapists to work with young people

Task 5.2: Rebuilding connections with your peers
Notes for the therapist

The aim of this task is to help the young person to start thinking about rebuilding connections with peers. It is important to encourage the young person to think about reviewing and re-establishing relationships that may have been fractured due to the illness. It is important to encourage the young person to have their voice heard and to have the confidence to follow their preferences within friendships and relationships, to help them recognise what their needs are and to seek the friendships/relationships that meet their needs.

Try to encourage the young person to think about the characteristics that they value about themselves and what characteristics they value in others. Also, try to think about how these characteristics manifest in behaviours and which they value and which they don't. For example, very popular friends might inhibit confidence and create competitiveness, which may not be helpful. In contrast, more playful friends could create fun and feelings of being carefree.

> **Guiding principles**
>
> Focusing on the concept of "generalisability" and how these principles can be applied to other areas of life.
>
> Acknowledgement of the way you select people into your life will be based on personal preferences and qualities that you truly value.

Task 5.2:

Create a list of activities that you could do with your peers that will help to rebuild and re-establish connections. Think about different types of friendships; those friends that you would like to share more with and those that don't need to know so much. Think about different types of situations and where you would feel more comfortable.

Notes for therapists to work with young people

Task 5.3: Respect your comfort zone
Notes for the therapist

The aim of this task is to help the young person to recognise when they feel pressure to conform when they don't feel comfortable. It is about helping the young person to understand that even though there may be specific pressures/stages in terms of growing up you can be independent and creative about how you approach these. So, enabling the young person to understand the discrepancy between individual development and societal/cultural development and how these can be very different.

For example, a young person's peer group may be doing different things from them. It is important that the young person is encouraged to see this in a positive way rather than seeing themselves as falling behind or as an outsider, enabling them to value the difference.

Guiding principles

Holding in mind the value of experience over achievement.

Challenging the idea that we should always push ourselves and seek achievement and there is only value in something that can be achieved.

Task 5.3:
Remember that it's always okay to not fit in. Respect your own comfort zone. Sometimes you can learn more about yourself by managing and respecting your comfort zone. Discuss with your therapist situations that may create conflict within. Problem

solve how to manage these situations remembering it's okay to not fit in. Develop your own self-soothing list of things to do when you are struggling.

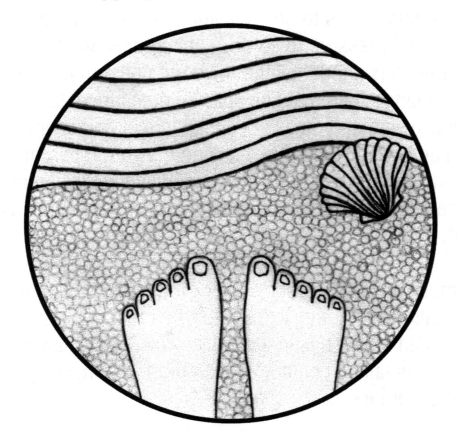

Task 5.4: Future aspirations
Notes for the therapist

The aim of this task is to enable the young person to engage in the idea of their future in a way that is not related to concrete goals or achievements and to focus on qualities and the way that things are experienced rather than outcomes. It encourages the discussion to move on to thinking about how different contexts/environments can enable the young person to express this through their behaviour.

Notes for therapists to work with young people

Guiding principles

Presenting a future that is not linked to achievement and goals.

Presenting the idea that meaning can be valuable regardless of the outcome.

Focusing on internal qualities of yourself and of the people around you.

Task 5.4:

Think with your therapist about your qualities or strengths, or the qualities or strengths that you value in other people. Then try to create your own wish list based on this. The wish list could be made up of words or images. Each group of words or images reflects different aspirations that you may feel are important for the future. Try to identify what you would need to keep doing and the things that you have learnt that can help you hold onto your wish list. To avoid the wish list becoming dated or irrelevant to your life, think about the things that are important to you as a person to keep it going.

You could start by thinking about the following sections:

- Your qualities and strengths
- Wish list
- Things to keep doing to keep your wish list ongoing and relevant to you

Notes for therapists to work with young people

Task 5.5: *Private place*
Notes for the therapist

The aim of the task is to create an impression of ending for the young person. Of course, it won't be a complete ending as personal development is a continuous process. The focus needs to be only on the person rather than referring to the illness. In this case, the therapist can explain the task but it needs to be private. The privacy must be respected as the point of the task is to illustrate that the young person can have a private place that does not need to be shared and where there is no judgement or evaluation from anyone.

Notes for therapists to work with young people

> **Guiding principles**
>
> We are all entitled to a "safe space" that can be private and not necessarily exposed.
>
> Introducing the idea that we can value the space because it is our own rather than something that is shared and validated by others.
>
> Promoting the idea of self-validation and ownership of the internal experience through this space rather than external validation.

Task 5.5:

Choose any style of communication you feel comfortable with. It may be writing a letter to yourself or a video only for yourself. This letter or video needs to represent a "private place" that you can access anytime, it does not to be validated by anybody else. The point of this task is to help you own your thoughts, feelings, dreams and aspirations or anything that has meaning for you. This will be just for you and the hope is that you can carry this with you through your life.

Laura's story

Meeting her own needs

Through the process of therapy, Laura was able to work on the discrepancies between her view and the views of others. She was able to see that sometimes being able to hold in mind the perspectives of other people can be a helpful way to see her struggles in a different light. Laura was able to involve members of her family to help her think about things that she could do differently and to be more open and honest with them in asking for help rather than struggling on her own. She acknowledged that being more open was a positive thing and that it could improve relationships rather than damage them, which was one of her most deeply rooted fears. Laura had been afraid to show her true feelings to her parents for fear of making them feel guilty. Once she was able to be more honest, the relationships improved and her parents were able to support her.

Laura was also very brave in terms of being able to describe to her family and friends the things that she did not find helpful. This was an important process as it allowed her to name these things and also allowed her to openly share them. Prior to the work, Laura would have struggled to assert herself with her family and friends for fear of upsetting them and so would have held onto all the negative feelings of frustration that she may have been feeling towards them instead of being able to work through them positively. She began to feel more empowered through this process.

Through this process of empowerment, Laura slowly but gradually began to rebuild her confidence and self-esteem.

Notes for therapists to work with young people

She realised that it is okay to do things differently sometimes, that you don't always have to fit in with something that doesn't suit you. She understood that there is a personal cost to trying to fit in when you don't feel comfortable and aren't happy to sacrifice her own personal needs to meet the needs of others. In quite the same way, Laura became better at being able to meet her own needs and not seeking out the reassurance of others in terms of being able to fit in. She realised that she could be comfortable making her own decisions, decisions that were good and positive for her and her own emotional wellbeing.

In terms of difficult conversations around weight Laura decided to:

Remove myself from these conversations and discussions, also if around my best friends, I can explain that I find this topic difficult to talk about as they will know what I have been through. I am not going to share anything that I don't want to share. I will have a pre-prepared answer for when I am asked where I have been.

Through the process of developing her own identity and self-esteem, Laura was able to think about her own strengths and qualities and what she needed to do to maintain herself and the things she needed to avoid stopping herself from struggling. As a result, she became more adaptable and resilient to change. She summarised her thoughts and feeling about this in a letter that she was able to read on difficult days.

Notes for therapists to work with young people

Dear Laura,
This is a letter that I want you to always read when things become too difficult. It has some important reminders and suggestions that could help you out.

The decision as to what happens to you is now up to you. You have put the things that were inside for too long on the table. Now don't let yourself keep it inside again. Tell someone. Do it for you so you will not fall back down.

You deserve to have a lot of joy and happiness in your life. Allow yourself to have this. Do something nice. I know how you like to watch a movie by yourself at night with some popcorn. Do that right now.

You also like to go to the beach. You like the smell of the nice fresh air and to hear the waves as they hit the shore. Why don't you take a walk by the beach tomorrow morning?

You love to draw and write fantasies. Maybe this would be a good time to do it. You always say how you feel able to just escape in your art.

Remember that there are so many people who love you always. Your mum, dad and grandparents are always here. You are not alone.

You are also not perfect either and that's okay.

You have dreams and aspirations that are valuable to you. You want to travel and go to France, Japan and India. You

Notes for therapists to work with young people

> *want to fall in love and have a family. You want to move to the countryside. There is so much waiting for you.*
>
> *Remember there is so much to fight for.*
>
> *With Love*
>
> *Laura*

Notes

1 Grosz, S. (2013). *The examined life: How we lose and find ourselves.* Random House.
2 Prochaska, J.O. & DiClemente, C.C. (2005). The transtheoretical approach. *Handbook of psychotherapy integration, 2,* 147–171.

Index

abuse: alcohol 26; child 101; substance 26, 101
achievement 22, 75–6, 105, 189–91; personal 101; social 97; sports 104
anaesthetic code 98
Anorexia Nervosa 4, 25–6, 61, 65; and Bulimia Nervosa 5, 26; focused family therapy for 7; focused psychotherapy for 7; and identity 46; prevalence of 5
anorexic: attitudes 85; behaviour 8; cognitions 135; forms 25; thoughts 77
anxiety 48, 118; as a comorbidity 6, 64, 76; coping with 75, 78, 82; and ecopsychology 109; and emotions 129; and identity 21–2; and a pandemic 101–2, 105; pathological 108; performance 108; and praise 94
attachment 34, 42
attunement 34–6, 50
autonomy: and attunement 36; and food intake 24–6; and gender 37; and identity 21, 46, 99; and praise 96; and sensitivity 98; and social integration 61

Binge Eating Disorder 4–5, 8; bingeing 4–5, 95
body: dissatisfaction 48; image 15, 43–4, 79–80, 104, 137
brain: changes 42; development 6
Bulimia Nervosa 4, 79, 161; and Anorexia Nervosa 5; focused family therapy for 7; prevalence 5; and psychological distress 26

child: ideal 96–7; sensitive 96
childhood: to adolescence 33, 39; and the anaesthetic code 97–8; and attunement and attachment 34; and emotional experience 15; and gender 36; and the ideal and sensitive child 96; and parental relationships 39; and parental separation 41
clinical: applications 32; supervision 4
cognitive: behaviour therapy 7–8; restructuring 7; symptoms 4
communication: and attunement 35; food and 38–9; skills 98; therapeutic 2; and therapist sensitivity 92
confidence 22, 44, 65, 95, 188, 194
confidentiality 4–5
control: achievement and 105; and autonomy 25–6, 62; and body image 44; emotional experience and 16, 47, 155, 157; emotional regulation and 48; filters and 22; and identity 61–2; and obsession 60, 84–7; and therapy 65; and weight preoccupation 75
cultural: influences 158; traditions 24; values 21, 44, 82

culture: and emotions 127; high-touch 91; integration into 96; and narratives 68; and sensitivity 30; and weight 77–8

dandelion and orchid metaphor 28–9, 52, 84; *see also* sensitivity
depression: and Bulimia Nervosa 26; as a comorbidity 6; ecopsychology and 108–9; and experience of therapy 64; and a pandemic 101
diagnosis 4, 9, 60; DSM-V 6
Dialectical Psychology theory 14
diathesis-stress model 15, 26, 28, 158
differentiation 14, 41
disorder-focused approach 6

ecopsychology 59, 108
emotional: awareness 20, 36–7, 45; belonging 19–20; development 39; expression 47, 124, 151; health 34; intelligence 81, 92; regulation 4, 7, 35, 38, 48, 139; understanding 10; vulnerability 18
emotional experience 9, 45–8, 87, 116, 119, 158, 169–70; and attunement 35–6; and childhood 34–5; connecting with 51–3; development of 34; gender and 37; internal 130; and narratives 41; role of 2; and sensitivity 15, 32; understanding 2, 10, 15–16, 46
emotions: expressing 2, 23, 132; experience of 47, 49 *see also* emotional experience; identifying 121–2; managing 15, 115, 161; negative 38; role of 16, 33–4, 52; sensitivity and 31–2
exercise 5, 23, 152 *see also* physical activity
experience: physical 3, 33; psychological 3, 43
expressed emotion 40

factors: biological 15, 36; relational 15; vulnerability 28
family: dynamics 42, 71–2; environment 25, 27–8; expectations 14, 85; involvement 41, 58, 71–2; therapy 7, 72–3; siblings 73
feedback 5, 64
filter 21, 53
food: culture 24, 59; experiences of 38; preferences 38

gender 15, 36–7, 40, 42, 77
guilt: and bulimia 26; and gender 36; and feeding 38; and identity 21; and keeping up performance 144; and praise 95; and psychological distress 20; and the sensitive child 98; and weight preoccupation 76, 85

hunger drive 4

Index

identity: narrative 40–1
impulse-control paradigm 6
independence 7–8, 18, 20, 25, 71
individualisation 145
individuation: and attunement 35; and identity 41, 171; need for 14, 17–21, 25, 143, 162, 186; process 14, 53, 117, 128, 164, 175; self- 61; and the sensitive child 98
inpatient 4, 9, 92; admissions in a pandemic 106; weight preoccupation 75

maintenance: cycle 50; factors 39, 48
malnutrition 6
management: stress 8; symptom 9–10; weight 3, 9
mentalisation 42, 81
metacognition 42
mother: -daughter relationship 36–7, 61; and narratives 40
motivation: approaches 79; and emotions 34; evolutionary 28; extrinsic and intrinsic 43; and identity 22; and praise 95
multidisciplinary: team 75; teamwork 3
mutuality 62

narrative: chaos 68–9; identity 40–1; and memories 115; quest 69; and resilience 103; restitution 68–9; and storyboards 149; value of 67–71
needs: basic 14, 16–18, 21, 24, 52, 158; emotional 36; individual 3, 9, 21, 53–4, 85, 128, 173, 183; social 3, 9, 21, 53–4, 128
NICE guidelines 3, 6–8, 64
nutrition 7, 60

objectivism 70
obsession 6, 60, 76, 81
obsessive-compulsive disorder 6

pandemic 59, 100–4, 108
parental: anxieties 97; expressed emotion 40; feelings 36; involvement 72; relationships 15, 37, 39 see also family, mother; role 71; separation 40
personality: and the ideal child 97; impulsivity 6; and individuation 18; perfectionism 6, 80, 82–5; and psychological distress 21; and sensitivity 14; in therapy 91
physical: activity 81 see also exercise; awareness 45; experience 3, 33; health 7, 23, 67, 78, 108; pain 10, 45; response 33, 45
praise 93–6

prevalence 5, 108
psychodynamic 9
psychoeducation 7–8, 123, 125
psychological distress 9, 71, 116; and basic human needs 14, 19–20; and identity 15, 21–2, 24; and a pandemic 102; and parental relationships 40; and sensitivity 26–7, 30
psychotherapy 97; adolescent-focused 7; of a pandemic 100
puberty 43
purging 4–5, 77, 95

realism 70
recovery 3, 6; and narratives 67–8, 70–1; and a pandemic 105, 107; process 115, 183; stages of 87–9
relapse prevention 7, 10; slipping 183–5
relationships: friends 107, 187–8; peers 23, 42, 93, 102, 105–6, 133, 184, 187–8
resilience 26, 94, 102–4

self: -awareness 20, 34, 37, 93, 117, 139–40, 178; -confidence 6, 44, 94, 98, 120, 136; -control 86; -criticism 4, 164; -development 3; -esteem 7, 44, 80, 94–5, 136; -harm 45, 81; -identity 33; -image 10; -monitoring 7; -objectification 48; -reflection 39, 47, 178; -regulation 14, 40; sense of 16, 33, 35–6, 46–7; -soothing 190; -validation 193
sensitivity: biological 27; differential 14–15; environmental 27–8; sensory processing 27, 29
social: acceptance 42; cognition 42; connections 18; construction 36; context 14, 36, 43, 98, 117; development 24; inclusion 42; integration 14, 16–20, 25, 61, 71, 143, 145; media 10, 22–3, 44, 51, 68, 96, 106, 117; modelling 18, 119; pressures 75, 180; relationships 16; skills 7; systems 17, 22, 32, 39, 96, 99
socialisation: gender 36; process 96, 128
Snapchat dysmorphia 44
spectrum model 6
stages of change 117
storyboard 138, 148–50
symptoms: behavioural 4; cognitive 4; psychological 82, 85; physical 82, 84–6

therapy: individual 72; fatigue 2; sessions 4, 72
therapeutic: alliance 7, 66, 77, 181; engagement 2, 4; rapport 91, 123; relationship 4, 11, 91, 125, 159; setting 63

Index

transdiagnostic approach 6
treatment outcomes 6, 67

validation: emotional 14, 46–7; external 36, 44, 47, 166, 193
violence 89, 101

weight: body mass index (BMI) 76; weight for height 76; management 3
wellbeing: adolescent 41; emotional 9, 195; psychological 17–19, 142, 184; physical 142